Bernard Darwin (1876–1961), fine amateur golfer and the greatest golf writer of them all.

"Writing about sport is worth nothing without gusto."
Bernard Darwin

THE CLASSICS OF GOLF

Edition of

MOSTLY GOLF

A BERNARD DARWIN ANTHOLOGY

Edited by Peter Ryde

Foreword by Herbert Warren Wind

Afterword by Donald Steel

Foreword

One of the hardest things a person can be asked to do is to step in and replace a man who has been in a class by himself, revered as peerless at doing what he did. For example, how unnerving it would be to be told that you were the person to take over for William S. Gilbert and write the lyrics for Arthur Sullivan's next score; or that Fred Astaire was washed up, and that you had been chosen to step in as Ginger Rogers' dancing partner in her next picture; or that it had been decided that Don Shula should be put out to pasture, and that you had been selected to coach the Miami Dolphins. Well, that was the position that Peter Ryde was in when in 1953 the Times of London named him as the successor to Bernard Darwin as its golf correspondent. What a pair of shoes to fill! Darwin had practically invented golf writing. He had been covering the game for the Times for forty-seven years with no diminution of his contagious enthusiasm.

The people at the Times made an inspired choice. They selected Peter Leighton Ryde, a chap in his late thirties, who had been with the paper for a number of years and had handled whatever assignments he had been given very ably. He was especially good at writing Fourth Leaders, light-hearted perceptions that followed the editorials. Peter Ryde—he never used his middle name as a journalist—had been educated at Charterhouse and at Trinity College, Oxford. In the Second World War, he served with the Royal Gloucestershire Hussars and the Fife and Forfar Yeomanry. After the war, he worked for the

Gloucestershire Echo *and the Manchester* Daily Express *before joining the* Times. *Ryde is an untemperamental, honestly modest fellow. When he was asked how it was that he was picked to be the* Times' *golf correspondent, he would explain that he didn't know—maybe it was because he walked into the* Times' *office some afternoons with a bag of clubs slung over his shoulders after a morning round, and that perhaps a few editors may have gotten the impression he was an ardent golfer. He was quick to add that he was only an average player, and that he had never got his handicap down into single figures.*

In those days when a good number of the British golf writers were such eccentric characters that the group was called "The Crazy Gang", Ryde stood out because of his serenity, his quiet charm, his amiableness with his colleagues, and the calmness with which he dealt with the pressures that a golf writer for a daily newspaper is under. Pat Ward-Thomas, who had his days when he was so disgruntled by the slowness of play or some other nuisance that he resembled nothing as much as Mt. Cotopaxi in eruption, once remarked of Ryde, "I don't understand Peter at all. He's so dispassionate. He's so English. I don't know how he is able to be so offhand day after day."

One thing that lay behind Ryde's equanimity was the sensible way he approached his daily chores during a tournament. After a morning of watching play, followed by a light lunch at one o'clock, he would repair to his hotel room, if it happened to be handy, or to a quiet corner of the press tent, and write several paragraphs about the morning's play. Then he would return to the course and seek out the right golfers to watch. At the end of play later in the afternoon, he finished his coverage of the day's high points. He was a shrewd observer and a thoughtful, graceful writer. I remember once asking Peter about how he went about his work, for I was impressed not only by the quality of his writing but by the genial manner he brought to a difficult job. "Well, once I discovered how helpful it is to get down to writing something about the morning's play after lunch," he said, "that made everything incalculably easier. Later you could make whatever changes you wanted to in your account of the morning's golf, and nearly always you had enough space to describe the afternoon's play in detail, if that was when the crucial shots were struck. Another thing I learned after four or five years was not to try to write a masterpiece. Just let it come the way it comes."

There are a couple of side notes about Peter that should be added. To start with, he has the ideal build for a golf writer. A good-looking fellow with pink cheeks, he is about six-two—tall enough to peer over a gallery crowded deep around a tee or a green and to see what is taking place. His writing, which was very sound to begin with, became remarkably acute and discerning. Gerald Micklem, the Sultan of Sunningdale and one of the top British players and administrators since the war, once appraised Ryde in the turbulent manner of speaking that he picked up neither at Winchester or Oxford, but perhaps at the Victoria Falls: "Peter, in a word, has provided the answer to the old riddle. He has demonstrated that it is easier for a good writer to learn golf inside-out than it is for a good golfer to learn to write capitally well".

Peter Ryde retired as the Times' golf correspondent

in the early 1980s, but he continues to attend the big tournaments and to do feature pieces for the paper. He has done several books. In the early 1970s he and Donald Steel—the writer of the Afterword for this book—collaborated in producing "The Encyclopaedia of Golf", one of the few indispensible golf books. "Mostly Golf", subtitled A Bernard Darwin Anthology, appeared in 1976 on the centenary of Darwin's birth. No one could have done it better. In 1981, Ryde brought out "Royal & Ancient Championship Records", the most attractive record book I know of. Along with the tasteful design of the pages and the artistry of the typesetting, these pages filled with scores are punctuated with occasional photographs of the leading players, with excerpts from contemporary writing about the nature of the game, with helpful historical notes about the changes in format of certain championships, and with a cartoon or two along the way. Ryde's most recent book is "The Halford Hewitt", the story of the annual tournament staged at the Royal Cinque Ports Golf Club, in Deal, in which the ten-man teams are made up of the graduates of individual public schools—what we would call private prep schools—and which by any name would seem to account for many more lifelong friendships than one makes at his college or university.

"Mostly Golf" is a wonderful book, one of the finest anthologies that I have ever encountered. Darwin, as you may already know, wrote on many other subjects besides golf. For example, he wrote two books about Charles Dickens, one about the landmarks of London, one in praise of public schools, and a biography of W. G. Grace, the famous cricketer, not to mention two childrens books. Of the forty-eight selections that make up "Mostly Golf", thirty-three are mainly about golf, though golf, like a curious child, peeps briefly into just about every piece. Of the other fifteen, three are about cricket, and one each is mainly about running, reading, field hockey, dogs, browsing, Dickens, Mr. Elisha Robinson of Bristol, Sherlock Holmes, boyhood fancies, fake sportsmanship, the leaf-catching game and the old game of chole, and the University Boat Race. I think it was a fine idea of Ryde's to include these non-golf pieces. They give the reader an idea of Darwin's other interests. But the golf is golf as only Darwin can write it. There are rather informally written but beautifully perceptive portraits of Gene Sarazen, Tommy Armour, Francis Ouimet, Walter Hagen, Joyce Wethered and Glenna Collett, Bobby Jones, Lawson Little, Harry Vardon, James Braid, and Ben Hogan.

One of the real highlights of this book is Ryde's long and absolutely brilliant Foreword. He tells us about Darwin and his lust for partisanship; the gusto, the superlative form of honest emotional involvement, with which Darwin approached most games; Darwin at work scribbling his dispatches in his spidery handwriting; Darwin talking out loud to Darwin in irritated tones while putting in the final of the Worplesdon Foursomes—it makes one laugh out loud; how Darwin would have hated the modern press rooms at the big championships (Ryde: "Where others today quote Nicklaus, Darwin, had he still been working, would have quoted Nickleby."); Darwin's unabated enthusiasm for golf (Ryde: "To mind about things is not a bad philosophy of life, however trivial they may be."); how well articles by Darwin that one has read and re-read still stand up

(Ryde mentions his stunning essay on Jekylls and Hydes); how, after beginning to write a weekly piece for Country Life *magazine in 1907, Darwin missed getting his copy in on time only one week down through the decades (Ryde: ". . . after making a rare visit to America, his dispatch failed to reach the office because the 'Mauretania was delayed by a gale.' "); how well Darwin knew Dickens' novels and how he could quote long, long passages from "Pickwick Papers"; Darwin's notorious verbal explosiveness during his golf matches, and his inability to stop himself from making witty but unkind remarks (Ryde: "And beneath it all was such kindness.") Ryde's insightful and rousing Foreword adds significantly to the worth of this Book.*

Herbert Warren Wind

MOSTLY GOLF

A Bernard Darwin
Anthology

Edited by Peter Ryde

ADAM AND CHARLES BLACK · LONDON

First published 1976
Reprinted 1977

A & C Black Ltd.
35 Bedford Row, London WC1R 4JH

© A & C Black Ltd. 1976

ISBN 0 7136 1687 3

Printed in Great Britain by
Hazell Watson & Viney Ltd,
Aylesbury, Bucks

Contents

Illustrations

Acknowledgements

I doubt if this attempt to refresh the remembrance of Bernard Darwin would have been possible without access to his writings in *The Times* and *Country Life*. To them for their help and encouragement my thanks, and in particular to *The Times* archivist, Gordon Phillips, and also to Darwin's literary executors, A. P. Watt. Others to whom I am greatly indebted make up a host of Darwin's friends and admirers of his writing. I cannot name them all—the names of some indeed I never knew—but I would like to single out Mrs Ursula Mommens, his daughter, Mrs Berta Ruck, his cousin, E. W. Swanton, who saw the possibilities long before I did, Raymond Oppenheimer, who lit up his humour for me and Gerald Micklem who, rather as Bernard Darwin had done, introduced me to the names of people who mattered. Colonel Tony Duncan, President of the Welsh Golf Union, Geoffrey Cousins, Vice-President of the Association of Golf Writers, Henry Longhurst, Leonard Crawley, Pat Ward Thomas, Lady Heathcoat-Amory, Roger Wethered, Andrew Macnair and John Cave have all in one way or another given me notable encouragement.

Just here and there I have taken liberties, as Darwin did in skipping Scott or skimping Dickens. I have compressed the original chapter from which 'The Best-Known Figure in England' is taken, because it seems to me to illustrate so well his ability to draw character. The book, which is to be reprinted with an introduction by John Arlott, is well worth reading in its entirety. For the same reasons I have taken similar liberties with extracts from *James Braid*. Older lovers of Darwin's writings may regard his words as sacrosanct and any interference with them as inexcusable. To them I can only apologise and ask them to believe that I have not been guilty of distortion and that my intention has been to try to whet the appetites as thoroughly as possible of those who are not familiar with his writings. In the case of his American trip, I feel that I am on firmer ground. His presence at the historic US championship of 1913 was the source of many articles from him—he was still writing about it thirty years later—and each successive article added something fresh to an event which took place before America's best writers on the game—Grantland Rice, O. B. Keeler and Herbert Warren Wind, to name three—had taken the field. It was only by welding these articles together into one piece, including both the events leading up to Mr Ouimet's victory and Darwin's reflections after the trip was over, that it has been possible to give for the first time a composite picture of that momentous event. For the rest, the anthology consists of pieces as he wrote them.

Peter Ryde

To Teresa

Some dates

1933	Won the Worplesdon Mixed Foursomes with Miss Joyce Wethered
1934–5	Captain of the Royal and Ancient Golf Club
1936	*Rubs of the Green* published
1937	Made a CBE
1953	Retired from the staff of *The Times*
1961	Died on 18 October

Foreword

Bernard Darwin was the great partisan. He was much more than that but his partisanship is the key to the magic and the freshness of his writing on sport for over half a century. Every game he watched or took part in assumed the proportions of an heroic encounter. As long as it lasted, and not a minute longer, nothing mattered except the defeat of the unspeakable enemy. 'Let us beat those beasts,' he said to his father as he trotted along beside him in a friendly foursome at Aberdovey. He was eight at the time but for the next half-century and more in every match that ever touched him whether as a rabid supporter of Cambridge or Kent or Wales, or in his own furiously fought battles on the fairways, that spirit of pugnacity continued to burn bright. So strong was it within him that one may imagine his approving the loyalty that burns, sometimes grotesquely, in the breasts of present-day 'fans' – a word he would never have tolerated. He would wear the appropriate tie as proudly as the supporters of Leeds or the West Indies or Arnold Palmer sport their mufflers and hats, though he would have abhorred the appalling manners of the wild fringe and been enraged by any action that interfered one iota with the fair run of play.

A striking example of his lust for blood occurred when he was taken by friends to watch Wales play the All Blacks in 1935. After dinner the evening before Darwin proudly recited the names of the entire Welsh XV who had beaten New Zealand in their first encounter thirty years before, and he no doubt threw in their initials, for he much preferred the use of these to the modern use of Christian names. (Halfway through the twentieth century it was still a bad bet to claim to know better than he the initials of the man who rowed No. 7 in the Cambridge boat of 1874.) The second match, in 1924, had been won by New Zealand so that special flavour was added to this occasion because it was regarded as the 'decider'. Not that extra flavour was needed by Darwin. The swelling chorus of *Land of our Fathers* coming from the packed stands at Cardiff Arms Park was enough to dim his eyes at once. Even judged by ordinary standards this was a match of great excitement; for Bernard it became almost unbearable. Wales were ahead, then narrowly behind as the last minutes were running out. A slip by the Welsh full-back – one can picture the scowl on that aquiline face – followed by a phenomenal drop-kick from the All Blacks' halfway line, caused him to cry out 'It's not fair, Wales cannot do it now, it's unfair,' and to jump up and down in anguish. He had never made any pretence of being a good loser, nor did he subscribe to what he called that 'anaemic rubbish' about the best man winning. He, or his side, must win. That was all there was to it. Then suddenly the tide turned again as Wooller's giant strides down the right wing made possible one last Welsh try. A hat followed others into the air and was lost for ever; whether he threw his own or that of a perfect stranger sitting in the row in front, as some aver, is not certain. It does not matter; the important point is that at the time he was fifty-nine and the only Welsh blood in his veins came from his maternal grandmother. On his own admission he was led away almost in tears.

On another great sporting occasion his emotions were stirred as deeply but in a different direction. Joyce Wethered's victory over Glenna Collett, the American champion, in the British championship of 1929 drew from Darwin a glowing tribute, but, as his article 'Ghastly, Horrible but True' illustrates, he suffered agonies before he could award her the palm. At one time in the morning round Miss Wethered, goddess of British womens' golf, was in danger of becoming six down; before she holed the putt that prevented her from doing so she happened to catch sight of Darwin. His face wore an expression, as she said later, that was a mixture of fury and dejection. Nobody in that vast crowd could have wanted more passionately for her to win. Whether he secretly wept tears of joy when she did win, one cannot tell. It would not have been surprising if he had, for he had the capacity to be deeply moved by purely sporting occasions. One of these was the Curtis Cup match of 1952 when everything depended on the outcome of the match between Elizabeth Price and Miss de Moss. Miss Price emerged victorious so that Britain won the cup for the first time, and in doing so holed a number of gallant putts. Darwin missed nothing of it and when it was over went across to where a colleague was sitting in his car, and spluttered through the window, making no attempt to hide his emotions: 'It was the bravest thing I ever saw.' He was dignified, wise, and courteous but on the fairways or round the touchlines of sport he became no ordinary zealot.

At the university match he suffered with the parents, hated to watch a good Oxford stroke, and was angered by a Cambridge failure. In his accounts he flavoured these feelings with humour and in describing how on such occasions old friends became avowed enemies, and in terming mere errors of judgement as criminal acts of folly, he was publicly admitting his own eccentricity and by doing so he made it acceptable. He thought that perhaps he should have gone to Oxford rather than to Cambridge, playing in its golf team as he did for as long as he was there. But the reason for this belief was not any lack of loyalty towards his own university. It arose from the fact that much of his home life was spent in Cambridge at the home of his grandparents after his mother's death. Cambridge was too near home, the contrast between term and vacation not sufficiently sharp. That was all. In all other respects Oxford University existed solely as an institution for being defeated by Cambridge. The torture and the ecstasy he suffered did not all come from golf; for some years he covered the athletics meetings between the two universities for *The Times* 'until I was sacked for gross partiality'. But whatever its source it appears slightly absurd to a generation which hardly knows when the fixtures are and does not even bother to turn out for the Boat Race.

His partisanship deserves one more illustration, much closer to home but none the less revealing. It shows, as do the extracts 'Lovelock's Mile' and 'Let The Better Side Lose' that if no reason existed for taking one side or the other, one had to be invented. Once, staying with friends, he returned from a walk with them and passing through the children's play room they sat down to rest. Two girls were playing ping-pong in a typically listless and haphazard fashion, or so it seemed to the grown-ups who went on with their conversation. Darwin did not join in the general talk, but after a while started to his feet and began to leave the room muttering. What had happened was that he had transferred his attention to the ping-pong. He could not be present at a match and not become involved in it. The player who was behind had begun to close the gap; she might have caught her opponent if she had taken her chances, but she kept failing to do so. Darwin simply could not bear it any longer.

It has been necessary, in trying to establish how much Darwin minded about games, to draw on personal, even intimate, experiences, because the depth of his feelings is not immediately apparent in his writings. There is a natural reluctance to air another's emotions, especially since the very mention of tears tends to make Britons uncomfortable. But readiness to tears is not necessarily a weakness or a fault. Berta Ruck, living still in the house at Aberdovey where her cousin used to stay, and two years short of a centenary for which Darwin himself is being remembered this year, does not recall him in tears in the childhood days they spent together, and her memory is wonderfully clear. In her opinion he was hard in character, but perhaps she confused that quality with shyness and reserve.

From whatever source this well of emotion sprang, it was most readily evoked, after literature, by his passion for the competitive game. In this he was following the tradition of those who had trodden the same path before him, and through whose pages he knew his way blindfold – Borrow, Hazlitt, Nyren, Tom Hughes, Nimrod, and, at the time of writing, he would probably have included R. H. Lyttelton and Neville Cardus. 'All these, unless I mistake them, felt intensely the romance of sport; they write about it as if they loved it, with that quality called gusto. Hazlitt has a short essay on Gusto, which he defines as "giving the truth of character from the truth of feeling, whether in the highest or lowest degree, but always in the highest degree of which the subject is capable..." .'

Gusto has nothing to do with superlatives. When there were great deeds and sensational incidents to report Darwin was at once on his guard. All his instincts of self-restraint, which were swept away as soon as he himself stepped onto the course to play, asserted themselves. It was in the smaller pieces, the matters of no account, that he had to exercise the art used by every essayist, and indeed by the best journalists, of writing bigger than life. Neither has gusto anything to do with gush. Darwin hated the back-slapper – 'fulsome beast' he would call him – and despised the writer who ingratiated himself with great players. But genuine feelings show through style and the reader is left in no doubt that the author was a man of sensitivity. Without it his writing, in spite of fluency and humour and the polish of scholarship might have given way to pedantry. An awareness of this amiable eccentricity seems essential to a better understanding of the greatest of writers on golf.

In 1907 there appeared in *The Times* an article, lugubriously entitled in the manner of the day 'Golf and the Championship'. It was the shallowest of headings, quite inadequate by modern standards to support the two full, unbroken columns that followed. The article is a milestone in sporting journalism. It marked the first step – a giant stride rather – towards a new conception of writing about sport in newspapers. Up to that time 'Sporting Intelligence' as it was still known in *The Times*, was little more than a jumble of figures at the foot of the page. By the time Darwin had finished with it, sports writing had blossomed into a branch of literary journalism.

That introductory article was not the first piece he wrote on golf. *Country Life* also claimed him about that time, and before he took either of these jobs he had been engaged by the *Evening Standard* to write an occasional column. All this happened in 1907, a red-letter year for him because it enabled him to sell his wig and gown and take to the fairways for ever. The championship referred to in the heading is not the Open but the Amateur championship. The amateur game was much the stronger of the two in those days although the presence of the Big Three – Vardon, Braid and Taylor – had already begun to swing the balance. But amateur events had always commanded more space than professional – not that either could get much of a foothold – and Darwin was simply continuing the tradition. It is in the 251st line of an article of 276 lines that the other side of the game gets a mention and then only with the guarded introduction: 'About professional golf there is really very little to say – Braid, Vardon, Taylor and possibly Herd, and there the story seems to end'. This dictum almost deserves to pass, along with other memorable aphorisms of his, into the history of the game.

His opening sentence is a reminder of changed times; for while admitting that golf is played all the year round, he says that it has a distinct season which was just beginning. The article is dated 23 May. It is difficult to realise now that apart from the Amateur there was little else that required covering. The four home championships did not exist, and the only international match of any kind was that between England and Scotland, in which Darwin took part with pride. The 'ladies' championship attracted so little attention that it had already taken place when he wrote the article and was not included in his vision of the season. The Amateur championship was everything and he was alarmed at the growing size of the entry. 'The list of entries is swollen by a number of persons with no conceivable claim to be rated as first- or even second-class players. The credit of having approached the position of scratch at small unknown clubs and over meadows bearing the courtesy titles of courses, combined with the wish for three or four days' cheap play over a championship course and with the chance of rubbing shoulders with the giants of the game, inspires an increasing number of players to cumber the ground by entering for a competition in which their legitimate part is as spectators only.' Elegance of style was never an obstacle to his saying what he thought. By modern standards there is more than a trace of snobbishness in the remark, but he was writing of the game nearly three-quarters of a century ago when, except in Scotland, it was the sport of the leisured and the well-breeched. It explains the presence in some of his writing of a touch of condescension in dealing with even the greatest of the earlier professionals, for whom it was still perfectly natural to enter the clubhouse through the back door.

In one respect times have not much changed since that article appeared. 'Scotland', we read, 'literally swarms with players who can come straight to the course from their plastery or plumbing and play a really fine game. Lack of experience is likely to prevent their winning outright, but they may oust some very good players in the earlier rounds.' Among the resounding names of John Ball and Harold Hilton and others who were highest in the realms of golf, one non-golfer makes his first appearance. It is a precarious entry for he is confined to the last sentence of all, but he came in later years to be accepted in every clubhouse in the kingdom. 'Nothing less would do that,' the sentence runs, ' "than a nat'ral conwulsion", to quote Mr Samuel Weller.' Those opening words in *The Times* were inscribed on the silver salver given him by a host of golfing friends on his retirement as golf correspondent forty-six years later. They are balanced by the last words he wrote, on the Halford Hewitt tournament in 1953, it being rightly judged that such a bewildering tournament was hardly one for his successor to cut his teeth on. That dinner, attended by Cabinet Ministers, judges, Governor-Generals, and men distinguished in almost every walk of life, reflected better than words his achievement over half a century. There was a feeling that *The Times* should have given him more recognition than they did, but this was a gesture they could hardly have undertaken except in a spirit of self-advertisement. Its greatest servants had always departed unsung; the retirement of Delane, the paper's most powerful nineteenth-century editor, occupied two lines at the foot of the column. In those days of anonymity Darwin could expect no other treatment. Even a banquet given by his colleagues in Printing House Square, so few of whom had ever set eyes upon him, would have been a hollow compliment.

He never trained as a journalist. In *Pack Clouds Away* he admits that after writing for newspapers for thirty years he knew wonderfully little about them, such knowledge as he had of their offices being largely gleaned from Sir Philip Gibbs' *Street of Adventure*, which, he added typically, 'is a book that I read about once a year'. He once described writing about sport as a job 'into which men drift, since no properly constituted parent would agree to his son starting his career in that way. Having tried something else which bores them they take to this thing which is lightly esteemed by the outside world but which satisfies in them some possibly childish but certainly romantic feeling'. The same holds generally true today; from Henry Longhurst, who started work selling advertising space in trade journals, down, the large majority had no firm intention of becoming golf writers before they first began to earn money that way.

If Darwin served no apprenticeship, he suffered no delusions that he was a professional in Fleet Street. On the rare occasions that he covered golf abroad he was vaguely alarmed at the prospect of sending off Press telegrams. In *The House that Fred Built* he describes how a French postmaster dotted the 'i's' and crossed the 't's' of a report Darwin wished to be dispatched, and having overcome the obstacle of the handwriting, remarked as he gathered up the sheets: "Ole, what is zees 'ole?' Darwin's writing was crabbed and spidery, his dispatches were scrawled on small sheets of paper, and pinned to a telegraph form franked for wiring to London at the night rate of eighty words a shilling. Geoffrey Cousins, a doyen of golf writers, remembers delivering some late copy of his own to the Hoylake Post Office one night, and being told on inquiring how the other copy was flowing: 'It's nearly finished; at least we've got rid of Darwin. Terrible writing. Sometimes we just can't figure it out and have to put in what we think he meant'. It was only later, when the services of Charles Macfarlane had been secured as a kind of Telephonist Royal, his bell-like tones sailing undeterred through the most scholarly passages, that the nightmares of telegraphists were diminished. In fact, Darwin's writing was not impossible; it needed a practised eye and a steady nerve; like a traveller crossing a gorge by a narrow plank, the reader had to keep steadily on without pausing or looking to one side.

Darwin had no truck with punchy introductory paragraphs. He thought the way to convey a picture of the day's play, and it no doubt suited him to think so, was to start by taking account of the weather, make a few general comments on the scene before him and on the state of the turf, and then take things as they happened. Having discussed the morning's play over luncheon, he would settle down afterwards, armed with a glass of port, and start writing – always, it seems, fluently, apparently easily and without faltering until he had finished. When Jock Hutchison holed in one at the 8th at St Andrews and rimmed the hole for a second consecutive one at the 9th, that unusual occurrence must take its proper place in the sequence of events, and if in the process it got buried halfway down the second column, that was no concern of his. When Sarazen took eight in the hill bunker at the High hole in the Open of 1933 Darwin omitted to mention the fact. One sentence, attributed to his writing about the 1934 Open, has passed into the history of golf writing; 'Then it was time to go to tea,' he is said to have written after watching the first two holes of Cotton's famous round of 65. I have been unable to unearth the evidence required, but there are several examples of his ending his piece with the words, 'As for the rest the results must speak for themselves'. Thus spake the essayist, intent on the quality of his piece, and on saying what he had to say. No criticism of his methods is intended; he is in any case beyond it, and he wrote not for a different generation so much as for a different century. The fact that so much of what he wrote has stood the test of time is a tribute to his quality no less than to the enduring virtues of the game.

Any shortcomings he may have had as a journalist were more than made up for by his first-hand knowledge of the game. He started playing at Felixstowe when he was eight, a slim figure in breeches and a white flannel shirt, insinuating himself between grown-up couples, endured by them only so long as he kept out of their way. In addition to his agonized victory with Joyce Wethered at Worplesdon (a more imposing event than it stands at the present) he won the President's Putter and the *Golf Illustrated* Gold Vase. Again both these events, in the absence of others at the time, ranked high in the list of achievements open to the amateur. He did not set himself up as a stylist. He complained in moments of bitterness that his style was too flamboyant and juvenile. A picture of him taken in his more active days shows a back-swing well past the horizontal, his left heel high off the ground to facilitate the full pivot, his whole position anticipating an explosive downswing.

He was probably too agitated a player ever to become a good putter and this may have prevented his reaching the top in the game. His opponent in that Worplesdon final remembers him muttering as he addressed the ball for a short chip from off the green made with an old cleek; 'Now then Darwin, come along Darwin, come along, keep it smooth,' and occasionally, 'Oh Darwin, you bloody fool'. The patter sounds like a remedy for an incipient twitch, especially as it was accompanied by a leapfrog movement of the clubhead behind and in front of the ball before the stroke was played. He had a peculiar horror, once he was in the lead, of the holes slipping away. Once, in writing about himself in the Worplesdon Foursomes, he described how, seized with the old terror of this happening, he went, 'weakly and weakly' into bunkers in front of his nose. The unique position he was in to write anonymously, usually disparagingly and always modestly about his own golf, was taken up in *The Times* by a correspondent, fully aware of the situation, who complained that the golf correspondent was unsympathetic and brutal in writing about a most worthy man and excellent golfer, Bernard Darwin. To read the paper, he never played a shot right in his life and was apparently suffering from every imaginable ailment in the second childhood of his life. *The Times*, the letter went on, made him sound decrepit, whereas the author of the letter had been pleasantly surprised to find him an upstanding man of early middle age wearing many clothes and a cheerful, if somewhat sheepish grin. But in the years of his prime amateur golf he was extremely strong, and he did reach the semi-final of the Amateur twice, managing at the same time, with the aid of trusty lieutenants, to send in lengthy dispatches to *The Times*. His concentration was no doubt fierce when he was playing, so that even the voice of Dickens was stilled within him, but the writer-player is seriously handicapped by the thought of what he has to do. A strong intuitive sense combined with vast experience also enabled him to read a match correctly on the flimsiest evidence. In the 1952 Amateur at St Andrews he overcame his dislike of hysterical crowds enough to accompany Bing Crosby for a few holes in his second-round match. Crosby started 3, 3, 3, and was three up, whereupon Darwin turned to the companion with whom he was sharing an umbrella and said: 'Well, that's all we need to see; he will lose by 2 and 1 or 3 and 2'. And he did.

As for the Press interviews on which so much sports writing is now dependent, he left an example of his attitude towards them after Max Faulkner had won the British Open at Portrush in 1951. The winner had come down to talk to the Press; Darwin endured it all for a bit, and was then heard to mutter as he rose to his feet and left the room, that what his readers were interested in, or ought to be, was what he thought of Faulkner's round and not what Faulkner thought of it himself. Hob-nobbing with professionals in order to make a report more colourful he viewed as odious familiarity, because it suggested an intimacy with the personality which was a source of pride. 'I think it is the football writers who are the worst offenders, or rather those who write

about them. Their wives and their twins, their houses and their
jokes are all served up to us with a sense of penny-a-lining gossip.
And worst of all, perhaps, their grievances and, but this applies
perhaps rather to runners, their excuses. I have heard an amusing
story about a baseball player who was called Alibi Ike. I wonder if
the title might not be revived.'

He would have viewed the elaborate Press centres of today with
abhorrence, glaring at the scoreboard covered in soulless figures,
and stumping out of the marquee at the anouncement of the next
player coming in to be interviewed. Where others today would
quote Nicklaus, Darwin, had he still been working, would have
quoted Nickleby. But to pursue the comparison further would
be to descend to fantasy. Darwin was moulded by the times
in which he lived. In his day a writer of golf had to forage
for himself. The bare figures were available to him when a round
was finished, but there was nothing to tell him who was leading,
who he should go and watch. There would have been nowhere
except his knee on which to rest his typewriter, so why should he
bother to learn how to use one? He did not drive a car, and would
not have wanted to add to his luggage which probably already
included his clubs and a present for the hostess of the private
house where he was going to stay.

One journalistic quality he possessed to an enviable degree. He
had the concentration to settle down and write his piece wherever
he had to. He strongly approved of trains and of the opportunities they gave him to complete an article. The most likely place
would be the corner of a lounge where, at the end of the day, the
most information was to be found. Not that he would have
needed to make much use of that. One pictures him slowly digest-
ing what he had witnessed in the course of the day; making
mental notes, for he never appeared to be writing anything down,
reckoning perhaps that what he did not remember would not
be worth reporting. He never tired of pointing out that he could
not be everywhere at once, and his advice to young writers was to
decide what was likely to be the most interesting round of the
day, and to go out and watch it. Whatever happened they should

write about the event, and if they could not make it sound the most readable event of the day, then they had no right to be doing what he was. What he preached he practised. He could make a 74 that he had watched sound more entertaining than a 67 which he had not. In the continuous freshness of his enthusiasm there is much to admire, especially in an age when television makes armchair critics of us all, and when over-exposure to sport numbs our sensitivity.

To mind about things is not a bad philosophy of life, however trivial they may be. And he did mind. His zest for the game drove him at the double from vantage-point to vantage-point, as long as he was physically able, just as, in earlier days, he had once ridden a bicycle for three from Trinity to Hunstanton, a matter of seventy miles, in order to take part in a match. Yet in spite of this he kept a tight rein on his emotions when it came to writing. He deliberately made every superlative earn its place. That is why his most enduring work – if we are to believe him, none of it was meant to be enduring – was in the quieter moments. His description of Horace Hutchinson, a golfer and writer whom he much admired, might be taken as applying directly to himself. 'He had the enthusiasm, the light touch, the power of pleasant prattle, the occasional and skilful discursiveness that go to make the agreeable essayist.' He never lost sight of the fact that golf is only a game and that there was a world outside it.

'To read of yet another dramatised version of Dr Jekyll and Mr Hyde is to turn instantly and with a sensible leaping of the pulse to the Stevenson shelf. "Heavens," we say to ourselves, "to think that we have not read it for ages. Why, it must be more than a year, perhaps even two!" To be sure we shall know it nearly by heart . . .'

In that brief effusion can be found the key to Darwin's life outside golf. It was peopled with books, samples of the classics which he came to love as dearly as his own clubs. It was an exclusive world. He was not a voracious reader of anything new, the walls of whose den would be lined with volumes. A few shelves only were needed to house the overworked books to which he remained, at times almost embarrassingly, faithful. This loyalty to his proven loves ran through his whole life. In the same way that he would prefer re-reading *The Wrong Box* to the adventure of trying a new novel, so one suspects he was never in a hurry to make the acquaintance of a new course. He was of course ready to accept the chance of visiting one. He was not so hide-bound as to turn aside from the chance of seeing Pine Valley, one of the splendours of American golf, where after seven respectable holes he started playing ping-pong back and forth across the 8th green and retired to the clubhouse. His pulse quickened as he visited Interlachen, the American course made famous by the lily-pad shot of Bobby Jones (a myth which Darwin was not slow to demolish) or the National Links of America where the eccentric founder of American golf, Charles Blair Macdonald, had held sway. But leave him alone with Aberdovey, Sandwich, the Old course at St Andrews, Formby, Deal or Rye and he would ask no more.

In general he preferred to find a fresh way of writing about an old favourite than to pay lip service to a new. 'Revisited' was a word which often found its way into the heading of a golf article, yet it never occurred to anyone to think that it would make dull reading. He had to do a good deal of revisiting in his writings, which extend over the first half of the twentieth century. In the long memories of the editorial staff of *The Times* certain passages of his began to ring bells. If he thought the passages written decades before would appear fresh to a new generation he was exercising what any journalist would consider to be his right, but it is probably no more than evidence of a tendency he had shown all his life, to till the soil he knew and loved rather than to break fresh ground. He played a great many literary rounds with the same set of clubs. His output on a relatively narrow range of subjects was prodigious. In addition to his day-to-day pieces for *The Times* his eagerly awaited golf column appeared Saturday after Saturday. In all those decades he missed only one week in *Country Life*, and that was in 1913 when, after making a rare visit to America, his dispatch failed to reach the office because the *Mauretania* was delayed by a gale. In his daily writings he came to rely less and less on the run of play and more on his ability to sketch personalities and write easily and pertinently about anything remotely connected with the subject. 'I have now for some years past earned a precarious living by writing golf articles with as low a percentage of golf in them as possible.' And he went on to advise the readers of *Green Memories* to read first the non-golfing parts which he described as decidedly the least tiresome.

His absorption in a few well-chosen subjects, and the amount of time taken up by playing and writing about golf, explains why he did not expand his range of subjects. The urbanity of his style and the conservativeness of his nature made him the right and obvious choice for works on the British public school and on British clubs. Eton and the Garrick, both of which institutions he loved, provided good background material for the slender, gracious books on those subjects. But however much one may applaud the public school spirit and the propensity of Englishmen to form themselves into clubs, as he did, it is a devilishly difficult sentiment to express in print. To an extent both the books reflect this difficulty, although the knowledge he reveals of great headmasters of the past makes a valuable historical document without even beginning to be dull.

With Dickens he was on surer ground; no one before or since, it is safe to say, has had a closer knowledge of his writings. Yet, although one might easily pick up a quotation from Sam Weller or Joe Gargery in an account of the Open golf championship, it is not easy to find a passage for all time in his writings on Dickens. In 1913 Lord Northcliffe commissioned Darwin to write a series of articles on the places Dickens had written about. It was with these fresh in his mind, perhaps, that Darwin, before he was banished overseas in the First World War to run an Ordnance depot in Macedonia, wrote the article 'Dickens in Time of War' which gets to the root of his love of that author, and which shows at the same time Darwin's mistrust of effusiveness and that passion for reading in all its aspects which were part of him.

Anyone who could have written that, and who could have taken on with complete authority an introduction to the *Oxford Dictionary of Quotations* of which that publication could be proud, could have written novels or biographies, or at least have become an awesome literary critic.

The source of this intimacy with classical literature lay in the thoroughness of his grounding in the subject. Books read and re-read, diaries faithfully kept, couplets composed for a domestic occasion were a more natural part of mid-Victorian childhood than they are now. All his life Darwin was at home with the written word. His daughter, Ursula Mommens, recalls with affection the times he read aloud to her, and to her brother and sister. His chosen passages were savoured to the full, and tears would come into the reader's eyes at the approach of a specially loved piece. Those moments were beautifully captured by his wife, Elinor, in a picture heading for a chapter in *Every Idle Dream*. This reading aloud was a habit handed down; his father had done it for him, conscious perhaps of the gap that needed filling after the death of the boy's mother in childbirth.

He set great store by this tradition of reading aloud. It is apparent in 'Freedom to Skip' and appears briefly in the leading article from *The Times*, 'Dickens in Time of War'. Elsewhere in *Every Idle Dream* he emphasises the importance to children that the colours of all the clothes in a story be precisely given. He turns to *Ivanhoe* to find an illustration of this: 'It is when Brian de Bois-Guilbert comes riding down the forest glade that Scott really lets himself go. From his scarlet cap laced with fur (scrumptious!) to his large two-handed sword, he occupies two pages. Second only to him in point of detail is Prince John caracoling round the lists at Ashby in crimson and gold and fur, "with golden spurs and such a tippet and cloak" – but I must not copy out all that lovely stuff as I should like to.'

Such enthusiasm is infectious, and it is not the least of the influences that he exercised that those who came under the spell of his writing were given fresh insight into the joys of literature. Not that he was uncritical. He knew, for example, the hazards of reading Scott and recognised the 'lamentable morasses of dullness' to be found in his pages, but skipping in a book – a more drastic exercise than skimming – was not insulting an author he loved; it simply made the author more lovable. It is small wonder that he carefully explored the pitfalls and benefits in reading to his children; by the same means a door had been opened for him to life-long pleasure that never grew dim.

His thorough familiarity with good literature paid off early in his life. When he went under escort from his first school, Summerfield outside Oxford, to sit for a scholarship to Eton – it was meant only as a trial run for he was no more than twelve – he was confronted by a question on his favourite book at the time, *Treasure Island*. He spent too long on the question but his thorough knowledge of the subject must have impressed the examiners for he was awarded a scholarship. Ever since in golf articles no less than in literary ones, the voice of Long John Silver has sounded. There were other books not far behind in popularity. *Pendennis* reminded him in its early chapters of his own early flirtations with the law; and *Frank Farleigh* was always in his top ten, although he was the first to deplore its indulgence in melodrama.

He never forsook his early loves. Decades after his examination triumph he could write: 'It is impossible that anyone can ever tire of reading *Treasure Island*. I have just been looking at the pictures once again in my dear old edition of 1885 in its tattered red coat.' Of all his books *Tom Brown's Schooldays* was the one he knew nearest by heart, the one on which he said he would most like to be examined. The literature of golf was not in his time so rewarding, and although he embarked on a technical book with George Duncan (from which the extracts 'Know Your Weakness' and 'Easing the Strain' are taken) he gave short shrift to the rising tide of instructional books that have flooded the market ever since. One or two books only earned the reverençe from him that he bestowed more freely in the outside world of books. He used to talk tenderly of taking down his dear, dear Badminton Library edition on *Golf* 'with trembling hands for fear that the binding might finally collapse, and the dog-eared and crumbling pages lie scattered about the floor'.

He said, no doubt with tongue half in cheek, that he thought it an affront that anyone should read a new book in bed. Bed was the place for old favourites, lovingly taken down again from the shelves, their well-worn pages and jackets no less than scars of the long service they had given. In the age of his upbringing this fierce love of books was not so rare. There were fewer of them, they were harder to get, and there were fewer distractions. But to have remained faithful even to childhood loves for three-quarters of a century marks the sentimentalist and the conservative.

Whole passages of *Pickwick Papers* he knew by heart, and he would test himself by seeing when he got to the foot of a page whether he could continue a sentence without turning over. His passion for *Tom Brown's Schooldays* is typical and throws some light on his own feelings. There is about it an air of tradition which he breathed all his life, and especially during his happy years at Eton, but it would be in keeping with all we know of him if what chiefly attracted him about the book is its air of honest pugnacity illustrated by the two fights in which Tom becomes involved: the thrashing of the bully, Flashman, and the encounter with Slogger Williams – the latter a well-handicapped match. It is perhaps not too far-fetched to suggest that in Tom's protective loyalty towards the weakling, Arthur, one may catch a glimpse of his own instinctive kindliness towards the young – everywhere, that is, except on the golf course.

The quotations that stamped every Fourth Leader he wrote and most of his other pieces were saved from the charge of pedantry by their unaffectedness. He avoided the obvious quotation but found an apt use for a phrase it would simply not have occurred to anyone else to use. 'All werry capital!' is a humorous expression but it does not add much to a piece of writing, yet readers came to look for such interpolations and to miss them if they were not there. The writer of one of the Fourth Leaders in *The Times* was once ushered into the presence of the deputy editor and told in the nicest possible way that, whereas any man was entitled to draw on the world of Dickens in his own writings, yet there was an unwritten law in *The Times* that any such quotations should be left exclusively to the one man who could put them to better and more natural use than anyone else in the world. This aptness was not confined to *The Times*; it permeated all his writing. In the book he wrote on the history of the old Southern Railway, he leaves it to Madame Defarge from *A Tale of Two Cities* to illustrate the long drawn-out preparations for D-Day. 'It does not take a long time for an earthquake to swallow a town. But when it is ready, it takes place and grinds everything before it. In the meantime it is always preparing, though it is not seen or heard.' It may not be the most comfortable of quotations, that is a matter of opinion. But it is safe to assume that it would never have occurred to anyone else to make use of it in that way.

His own writing reflects in more ways than one this fascination for Dickens. He shares the same unaffected enjoyment of life, he indulges in the same ecstasies of sentimental memories of which 'The Jolly Dog Club' and 'Put Her In the Woodshed' are obvious illustrations. Above all he seems to have learned from Dickens the art of drawing character. It comes as something of a surprise to find that after experiencing the thrill of so many great matches and memorable championships and knowing how keenly he felt their impact, he has left behind so little writing in the grand manner – humour, understanding, faithful recording, yes, but so seldom the purple passage. The reason is perhaps that, since he could not trust his unruly emotions, when he came to pen his thoughts he kept a tight rein on them, disciplining them more sternly than he might otherwise have done.

By contrast his portraits of individuals are among his finest passages. Vardon, Braid, Sarazen, Armour, Hogan – the difficulty has been to know whom to leave out. Nor is his gallery confined to golf. His award of the C.B.E. in 1937 was for services to literature as well as sport. His knowledge of the former, though limited, went as deep as it is possible to go in his chosen authors.

The condensed chapter on W. G. Grace is a classic study of closely observed character. There are plenty of other examples outside sport altogether. When he comes to people he is matchless. He had cause to be grateful to the Lord Northcliffe of his day, for it was he who sent him to America and also allowed Darwin to accompany him on a golfing tour in the south of France, but he acknowledged that, and the few lines with which he described him are as balanced and generous as any he wrote. 'He seemed to me to enjoy with an innocent vanity his knowledge of the habits and customs of foreign countries and the impressing them on other people. It has often been pointed out that he took an interest in everything, which had in it something childlike, in that a child has not imbibed the fatal error of being bored. He liked, I think, to believe anything interesting, even though his more critical judgement might tell him that it was probably not true. He made one ashamed of feeling blasé because he found everything so intensely interesting and made it so for others by his own eagerness. A little of him might go a long way but it was a wonderful stimulant.'

No less observant are his remarks about his Eton tutor, the late Edward Impey: 'He knew, I feel sure, that schoolmasters can acquire certain characteristics which frighten the outside world and did not mean to fall into that trap if he could avoid it. So he would take some pains to cast his pedagogic skin. I have a distinct vision of him sitting at the cricket in Upper Club on the afternoon of the Fourth of June. He has got rid of the parents or at least the worst onrush of them, at lunch, and now, when everyone else is in tall hats and white ties, here is my tutor in an elegant, grey "change suit", a straw hat and a Rambler tie, looking extremely dashing and handsome, disguised as a private citizen.

'I believe he was a very good schoolmaster indeed, very fond of his boys, and though perhaps through some deep, internal shyness not always quite at his ease with all of them, most sympathetic and understanding. Looking back I am sure that certain boys must have roused him to a white heat, as certain of his colleagues unquestionably did, but generally speaking he kept a noble control of himself. There were in his pupil-room two of the stupidest boys that it is possible even in a nightmare to imagine, but he treated them with a gently humorous patience that was a model.'

From every direction examples of this facility for bringing people to life could be given. His easy use of everyday words has the effect of making us feel we are in the presence of his subjects. He could sketch in a figure with the lightest of touches, as, when in speaking of that redoubtable Scottish golfer of his time, Mure Fergusson, he said that when he set off to retrieve a ball from the middle of a wood he managed to give the impression that he had struck it there on purpose. From the material he was provided with he gave the first head of the Bristol firm of E. S. and A. Robinson an almost Dickensian flavour ('Elisha the Founder'). One last sample from his gallery must be allowed, the picture he left of Nain, his Welsh grandmother who transferred the full weight of her affection on the death of her daughter to the motherless boy.

'Nain could hate a rogue, though she could make many allowances, and I do not think she liked a Whig, but she certainly did not hate a fool, for she was angelically kind to many such. But, indeed, I do not think "hate" is the right word for her at all, because in so many of our hatreds, or in mine at any rate, there is something mean and petty and Nain could not conceivably have been petty. She was of far too lofty a stature for that; those whom smaller people hated she would simply have dismissed, passing from the subject with a quiet and unapproachable dignity. If a single adjective had to be chosen to describe her, then there is only one that is possible – noble. She was the noblest creature that I have ever known.' Have more generous or understanding words ever been written by old boy or grandchild?

This warm affection for mankind lies behind the unfailing charitableness with which he wrote about golfers, and it brings us to the strangest paradox in his make-up – his behaviour when he himself was playing.

Darwin's behaviour on the course may not have enhanced the pleasure of those who had to endure it, but it had two redeeming qualities; it seldom lasted longer than the match itself, and the accounts of it, which lost nothing in the re-telling, added much to the general gaiety of living.

Once during the President's Putter, a tournament for which in those days the best amateurs in the country entered, he suffered a piece of atrocious luck at a crucial stage of his match. On the hard ground his good tee shot bounded away off the frozen green; his opponent's moderate stroke, following a bagatelle course, bumbled onto the green and finished close. Darwin cursed the hole, he cursed the course (Rye, which he loved almost above all others) and then, rounding on his opponent, this otherwise most courteous of gentlemen shouted: 'And, furthermore, Speakman, God dam' you!' His opponent, an ageing and mild-mannered schoolmaster, was heard to remark later that he had never before had the honour of playing with Mr Darwin but that he was bound to admit he found him a most uncivil gentleman. Undergraduates, to whom Darwin in their day addressed more words of encouragement than did any of their supporters, stood in awe of him on the first tee.

One such couple, learning that Darwin would be in the foursome opposing them the next morning, discussed the proper way to address the great man. One thought 'sir' would be safe; the other disagreed on the grounds that Darwin might consider it too subservient. On the first green next morning Darwin missed from a yard, and a voice rang out on the bleak morning air, 'Oh, bad luck, Darwin.' Darwin hated receiving sympathy, though he was generous in giving it, he hated missing yard putts, he hated losing a hole to two whipper-snappers. 'We had', said the partner who had held his tongue, 'a most uncomfortable morning.'

On the course he cared too much. This is the judgement of one who had plenty of time to study him, his partner in the Worplesdon Foursomes of 1933, Lady Heathcoat-Amory, as Joyce Wethered had by then become. She won that event eight times with six different partners. Darwin was her sixth partner. She must have known what she would be in for, because stories of Darwin's eccentricities on the course were universal. If she had any doubts about agreeing to play with him they were dispelled by her recollection of what she owed him in the early days of her golfing career. Hers was not a long apprenticeship in golf; she burst upon the scene with great suddenness. Contrary to what her record suggests, she was sensitive and shy and inexperienced. She was not used to company, and it was Darwin who helped her, not so much on the course – for she had nothing to learn there – as off it, by his helpfulness and encouragement. She caught something too of the joyfulness he found in the game and of his thirst for victory.

'A family foursome would be fought as fiercely as a public match. The day we entered for the Mixed Foursomes in 1933 I admit to having been really terrified of letting him down. I can still see him putting doggedly with his mashie after angrily discarding his putter.'

When she had a specially difficult approach to make over a bunker to a well-guarded flagstick he would stand, where he could be seen, with his back to her and his eyes hidden in his hands. On any count this is bad manners, but when it comes from one who was better mannered than most and when it is directed to one whom he recognised as the best woman golfer in the world at that time, and probably at any other, it is clear that we are in the presence of a golfing fanatic.

There are countless other examples of this fanaticism, of his going down on his knees and invoking the Deity at Woking, of confiding to a stranger at Deal his unprintable opinion of the partner through whose fault they were going to extra holes and who had foozled his drive to the 19th. He became a Demon King as soon as he set foot upon the fairways with a club in his hand. It was not a question of exhibitionism – his whole upbringing is against such an interpretation – it was as though he could not help himself. He grumbled and muttered, and swore at his own shortcomings. Lady Heathcoat-Amory was ready to forgive him. 'It was all worth while enduring,' she wrote at the time of his death in 1961, 'for the stimulation of his companionship, his conversation and his ability to make the day on the links stimulating and exciting. And beneath it all was such real kindness.'

He did not suffer fools gladly and was capable of making waspish remarks. One example of this I came across soon after taking over his job, in 1954. The first Commonwealth tournament had taken place and all the teams had moved to Muirfield for the Amateur championship. There in front of the forbidding bow windows of the clubhouse, Darwin came across one of the members of the Canadian team wearing a lumberjack shirt of large and brilliant checks. 'Tell me,' asked Darwin, 'are those your old school colours or your own unfortunate choice?' Rude? Yes, if you like, but there was a twinkle in his eyes when he said it – his eyes could twinkle – that banished bitterness.

Yet on the rare occasions when he criticised in print he did it with all the gentleness and consideration of which a sensitive writer is capable. It needed to be well deserved before even the driest and mildest of reproaches could be drawn from him. Young golfers from Miss Wethered down have acknowledged the help they received by the warmth of his encouragement and his understanding of their feelings.

Another aspect of his regard for the individual and his feelings was related to me by a fellow writer who came into the job in Darwin's last few years. My friend was asked his opinion of a certain well-known golfing figure, and with some reluctance gave an honest and none too favourable reply. Darwin contrived it that they both left the room together, whereupon Darwin said: 'Do you mind if I give you a piece of advice? It is unwise in my opinion ever to say anything derogatory in public about anyone.' It was a friendly act meant entirely for the beginner's own good. Or course 'in public' also includes the columns of a newspaper, and it was extremely rare for Darwin ever to say anything unkind in print. My experience at his hands when I took over his job was one of unfailing kindness. He could never quite believe my handicap was as high as I said – I believe he thought that nobody should really write golf for *The Times* over a handicap of four – but he gave me nothing but help, introducing me to 'the people who matter' with a kind word, when he might have so easily done nothing and in so doing have left me a very uphill job.

Yet no one was in a better position than he to criticise where golf was concerned, because he had been 'out there himself'. He had captained Cambridge, played for England when the amateur game was at its strongest, and won his single in the first Walker Cup match against America when the British captain had been taken ill. Indeed he reached the highest position golf has to offer, that of captain of the Royal and Ancient golf club. Yet the man and his warmth of heart proved the stronger influence. The man who, as captain of the Rules of Golf accepted the responsibility of piloting a revised code of rules through the committees, and in so doing sowed the seeds of co-operation with the United States which have borne fruit ever since, was also the creator of *Ishybushy and Topknot* and *Oboli Boboli*. The links with childhood were never quite broken, and these nursery books which he wrote gave him the chance not only to delight a grandchild but also to give his wife, Elinor, an opportunity to show her talent as an illustrator. He loathed being a real soldier but never lost the fascination for the detachments of lead soldiers his military uncles had brought home to him as a boy. In later years it was not counting sheep that sent him to sleep but sending processions of soldiers through his mind in freshly invented uniforms.

Another of his passions, for none of his likings were half-hearted, was for murder trials, and although it would be too far-fetched to imagine a sense of rivalry between criminal and victim – that were altogether too one-sided a match – it is permissible to read into his interest for the subject generally that love of the matching of one man's strength against another, in this case that of the plaintiff against the defendant in the court room. There may also be reflected in that passion – it was so strong that he got his host-driver to break a journey between London and Southport at Rugeley in order to inspect at first hand the place where Palmer the poisoner lived – something of blood-thirstiness, finding expression in his own life in a certain vindictiveness of spirit.

No ordinary writer on sport could hope to claim the attention of following generations. This is especially true of day-to-day writers of whom Darwin was the most eminent. All daily writing is, or should be, ephemeral, and most ephemeral of all is writing on sport. Sometimes excitement and quality reach such a pitch that the echo of them lasts, but most accounts soon cool and are later read with a dulled eye and a lazy pulse. Darwin's writings, of which the samples on the following pages claim to be no more than a fair cross-section, must speak for themselves. A second eleven could be fielded, capable at least of making a good match of it against the first. The writer himself had no illusions about what he was doing. He certainly was not writing for posterity, and even his most solid pieces ring with deprecating expressions, recognising how easy it was for even the expert witness to get it wrong. But what is indisputable is the effect he had on sports writing. There were writers on sport before him whom he was the first to acknowledge, but no writer for a daily paper had noticeably trodden the path of eminence before. He blazed the trail. That others who followed made names for themselves only enhances the value of what he attempted. For Darwin, wrote a reviewer of one of his books, the public school man was the Englishman intensified. We who read Darwin now may find in him the golfer intensified.

My First Open (1908)

I have no desire to be cast upon the scrap heap, but the notion of watching an Open just once as an idle spectator with nothing to do is, I admit, a seductive one. Let people believe it or not, the reporting of that last day in particular is no joke, especially if you have two accounts to write and a broadcast or two thrown in. In my ears, as I think of it, is a confused sound of the rushing of crowds, the pattering of rain, the shouting of stewards, and the clicking of typewriters. I see myself, cowering in a shelter, asking imbecile onlookers for information which is never true, staggering back to the club-house for dry clothes, writing on my knee under the lee of a sandhill and having the paper blown out of my hand by a playful wind, looking at the cards pinned up in the Press tent and trying to invent some interesting manner in which the scores may have been arrived at. When a friend with nothing to do but relapse into a drink asks me how I 'get my stuff off', and whether I post it, I could do anything to him that is sufficiently malignant and has for choice boiling oil in it.

It seems to have become harder work since I first embarked upon it, partly because I have grown older and lamer, partly because championships have grown bigger. My mind goes back with yearning to the first Open that I ever saw and reported, that at Prestwick in 1908. I have forgotten the writing about it, which I took in my comparatively youthful stride, and remember only the fun of it. It seems to me, perhaps inevitably, the pleasantest championship I ever watched. The weather was fine and hot and sunny, the course green and lovely after a deluge of rain on the Saturday before; I stayed with kind friends right on the course, looking out on the Goose-Dubs from my bedroom window. It was ten years since I had first played in an Amateur championship, but this was my first Open (I never was so rash as to play in it); it was all fresh and exhilarating; I was still rejoicing in a new life and in a new freedom from thraldom of the law. Finally I saw golf played as well as I have ever seen it played since and, as it then appeared, incredibly well, for that was the year in which Braid won with 291, and only once before had the winner's score been under 300.

Apart from the tremendous nature of that score I suppose this could not be called an exciting championship, because Braid was winning easily all the time. Even when he took his famous or infamous eight at the Cardinal in the third round he finished in 77, and his nearest pursuers, already faint and far away, scarcely closed the gap at all; some of them even fell farther behind. Apart from that eight and the general magnificence of the winner I have grown rather hazy and, even though I have just read the account in the *Golf Year Book* of 1909, I do not remember as much as I ought, though certain things do come back.

James started in such a way as to make it perfectly clear that he was going to win. He began with two threes, went out in 33 without the ghost of a slip, and finished in 70. When we came back to the club, open-mouthed from watching this round, we found that it did not lead the field, for Ernest Gray of Littlehampton had done a still more astonishing 68. Gray was a fine player and on his day really brilliant but, with all possible respect to him, we felt that he was one of those who would 'come back to his horses', and in fact that was a sound prophecy, since the next best of his four rounds was 79. Those who were assumed to be Braid's most dangerous competitors, Vardon and Taylor, were already nine strokes behind him after one round; so was Ray, and though Sandy Herd had played very finely he was four behind; Tom Ball ultimately destined to be second, had taken 76. In short, it seemed as the Americans say, 'in the bag', and Scottish patriotism rejoiced accordingly. It had still further cause for rejoicing after the second round. This time Braid began quietly 4, 4, 5, letting a shot slip at the tiny little 2nd hole. After that he went sedately mad with four threes in a row; he was once more out in 33, home in 39, round in 72, and five strokes ahead of all the world.

Looking at the figures, I observe that in this second round he has a three at the 12th hole, and that brings something back to me; in fact it brings two things, a tremendous brassie shot followed by a long putt, and the only occasion on which I ever saw the sage of Walton so far demean himself as to run. The long since departed stone wall then guarded the 12th green and ordinary mortals played their seconds short of it and so home with a pitch. This time Braid had hit a very fine tee shot, rather to the left as I see it in my mind's eye, and took a long reconnoitring walk forward. It was then that, having made up his mind, he trotted or ambled gently and with no lack of dignity back to his ball and lashed it home. Oddly enough this desperate feat had, as its immediate reaction, the only serious mistake that he made throughout the four rounds, apart of course from the eight at the Cardinal. He frittered away the spoils of that three by taking a six at the Sea Hedrig. How he did it I do not remember, but accidents can always happen on that fascinating little pocket handkerchief of a green perched among the hill-tops. Immediately after that he got another three, at the Goose-Dubs. No doubt he holed a putt; the number of middle-length putts which he holed was appalling.

It was next morning in the third round, which is generally deemed the most crucial, that the eight happened, and by this time every earnest student knows how it happened – a second from a not very promising spot into the Cardinal and then two mashie shots, over-bold perhaps and striving for distance, which sent the ball glancing off the boards and out of bounds into the Pow Burn.

Apart from that horrid spectacle, I remember, or I think I remember, two things clearly. The only sign that James was a little shaken came at the 4th hole; he put his second on to the green and took three putts. At the Himalayas came glorious amends, a putt holed for two. I see it a little down-hill and from the right, but I daresay I am wrong; James doubtless recalls it with perfect accuracy. What I remember beyond all question is how we all broke into rapturous clapping. The crisis, in so far as there had been any crisis, was past. He was out in 39, home in 38; he was six strokes in front, and the eight had done no more than keep his pursuers just within sight of him. His last round was a model of confidence and steadiness combined and he beat Tom Ball, who ended with a 74, by eight shots.

The looking back at the scores has perhaps swept me a little off my feet into reminiscence. If I have been tiresome I apologise on the inadequate ground that I have myself enjoyed it. I have felt once more in imagination the Ayrshire sun on my back, climbed with eager steps the Himalayas, sat on the soft dry turf, behind the Alps green, and watched Braid moving stately and processional towards inevitable victory.

The Knot in the Handkerchief (1929)

Our Ryder Cup team, after a hard course of tournaments, have now vanished into a mysterious and exciting seclusion. I gather that they are at Harrogate. Whether they are drinking waters with 'a wery strong flavour o' warm flat irons' I do not know, though there would seem to be something vaguely appropriate in it if they were. Whatever their precise form of training, I feel tolerably sure that they are not, occult from the public eye, practising with handkerchiefs tied into knots.

It is perhaps too late in the day to suggest it to them; yet a gentleman of my acquaintance has found in this apparently simple device the twin secrets of driving and happiness. He had played golf of a kind for years before he was suddenly smitten with a desire for indoor self-improvement. Fluffy woollen balls and India-rubber balls brought him no relief; then he tied the knot in his handkerchief, shut himself up with a library of textbooks, and emerged after a time a creature changed and radiant.

I went to see him in his office the other day, that he might show me how it was done. It was a solemn moment when he took from a drawer a large plain white handkerchief. He rolled it up until it looked like a very long attenuated sausage. Swiftly and surely he tied a knot in it, and yet another knot, and now it resembled – more or less – a golf ball with two aeroplane wings attached. He repeated the process with another handkerchief, and our supply of ammunition was complete. Then he hesitated a moment. However, it was past one o'clock, there was no one about, and even a senior partner can do what he likes with his own luncheon hour. He picked up a driver from the corner, and stealthily we crept out on to the landing. Not a mouse stirred behind the wainscot; all was well; he put one handkerchief on the ground to act as a tee, the aeroplane wings pointing in the direction of the imaginary hole. Finally, with the air of a priest taking the sacrificial knife, he grasped his driver. I retired to the safety of the staircase to look on.

At this supreme juncture there came a most untimely interruption. Steps were heard on the staircase – the steps of Miss Somebody returning to work after all too short a lunch. 'Come along, Miss Somebody,' said my friend blandly, as if he were doing the most ordinary thing in the world, and with an embarrassed smile she plunged through the nearest glass door. Silence reigned once more, but only for an instant. Bang! there came a noise like a pistol shot. He had swung his driver round his head and the handkerchief had hurled itself against the wall. 'There!' he called proudly, and I, like Mr Wemmick's aged parent, when the cannon went off, exclaimed: 'He's fired! I heerd him!' But I had missed something of the point. The striker's exulting gaze was directed not at the handkerchief against the wall, but at the other one upon the ground. There it had remained, immovable and untouched, even as the face of the trusting spectator's watch from which Kirkwood drives his ball. The achievement was complete.

After that we went to lunch. I carried away with me one of the handkerchiefs tied by the master hand, and shall no more dare untie it than I dare unroll my umbrella when an artist has rolled it for me. I have, however, ventured to hit it, because before writing this plain and unvarnished tale I thought I ought to have a little trial on my own account. I admit, however, that I feel cramped and frightened in the drawing-room and so began by taking it on to the lawn. It whizzed away satisfactorily enough, but I could not make quite the same splendid bang with it as its creator had done. It may have been my puny hitting, or it may be that the real reverberating sound can only be obtained within four walls.

I may seem to have written lightly, almost frivolously, of this adventure, but in fact the knot in the handkerchief is, I believe, a capital device. One thing is certain, that it is much better to practise swinging at something than at nothing. When we swing merely at the empty air we may look like all the photographs of all the champions, and get our knees and our elbows into exactly the right places, but there is absent one intensely important element – namely that of timing. With nothing to aim at, we are much more likely – and Heaven knows we are likely enough when there is a real ball – to hit too soon. 'Wait for it' is one of the eternal imperatives of golf; we cannot wait for nothing, but we can wait for a handkerchief.

I cross-examined my friend rather sternly about hooking and slicing, since it seemed to me that he might be acquiring bad habits in one of these two directions without knowing it. He made some admissions but came back to the solid, satisfying fact that he had found out how to drive a golf ball after being unable to do so for almost unnumbered years. I only wish I had half his complaint. Crash! Bang! That was the genuine note. I have left that blessed handkerchief in the hall, and somebody else has had a shot at it. It sounds – it really does sound – as if he had broken something.

The Man from Titusville (1932)

' "All right", said the Cat; and this time it vanished quite slowly, beginning with the end of the tail, and ending with the grin which remained some time after the rest of it had gone.'

When I read my *Alice in Wonderland* and come to that sentence about the Cheshire Cat, I think of Gene Sarazen. His grin is so very much an integral part of him, and even when he has dashed away after winning our Championship to win that of his own country, he leaves an agreeable appearance in the air, resembling a grin, to remind us of him.

It is by no means an unchanging grin, as was that of the Cat. It grows perceptibly broader as he holes a long putt at a crucial moment, seeming then to spread entirely across his pleasant olive face. It contracts into something of a wry smile when the putts just decline to drop and he has perhaps hard work to keep smiling at all. It is, however, impossible to think of him without it, because it is the outward and visible sign of the very charming and at the same time very strong and resolute personality that is Sarazen.

I first met that grin in a hotel in New York in the autumn of 1922. Its owner had leaped into sudden fame earlier in the year by winning the Open championship at Skokie, a Chicago course. He then came from a course called Titusville. Nobody here had ever heard either of it or of him and even in his own country I do not think his fame was as yet very great. He soon proceeded to show that his win was no fluke, for he won the Professional championship of his country and beat Hagen in a set match over 72 holes, a thing that at that time no other golfer in the world was likely to do.

It was with the glory of his championship still upon him that he first came over here, in 1923, to play for our Open championship at Troon. His golf at once made a great impression on all who saw him. Arnaud Massy is capable of enthusiatic outbursts of hero-worship, and I remember his declaring that the championship was over before it had begun, since nothing could prevent Sarazen from winning by strokes and strokes. And then, by some astonishing accident, he failed to qualify. He had a bad first round, but played up gallantly in the second and was believed to have saved his bacon. I remember it well because after dispatching my telegram saying that he had qualified, I had departed far from Troon. Next morning I was horror-stricken to hear that someone had come in at the last moment and ousted him. Fortunately, there was a trusty person in London who had altered my message or furious editors would have had my head on a charger.

When we saw him after an interval of nine years at Prince's playing the sort of golf that seemed incapable of going wrong, it was almost impossible to believe in that earlier failure; but in the first place he was then nine years younger, and decidedly more 'temperamental', and in the second, allowance must always be made for the strangeness of a strange land. When Bobby Jones first played in our championship he tore up his card and drove his ball out to sea; when Hagen first played he finished in something like the fifteenth place. It is hard work to play a game in the other fellow's country, and it seems that a probationary visit is needed before even the greatest can give of their best. However it happened, Sarazen accepted his downfall very well and declared that he would come again if he had to swim across. He had to come again several times, but the long lane had a glorious turning at last.

Even in his own country Sarazen's golf suffered for a while a period of partial eclipse. I fancy that having at first played the game almost entirely by the light of nature he took to thinking about it. That is a thing that has almost got to happen to any good young golfer at some time and occasionally the young golfer is never so good again afterwards; the 'first fine careless rapture' of hitting, the splendid confidence are never satisfactorily replaced. If on the other hand he gets safely through this inevitable distemper he is a better golfer than ever he was, for he has knowledge to fall back on in evil days. Sarazen, I believe, tried experiments. He tried for instance the fashionable overlapping grip instead of the interlocking one that had come to him almost instinctively in his caddie days. I think in the end he did make some slight change for I remember his asking me when we met again if I saw anything different; I had to confess that I did not and asked humbly to be told. At any rate the period of thoughtful sickness was safely passed and there emerged a Sarazen who, though he did not win another Open championship till this year, was yet a better golfer than before. He was always there or thereabouts, and I imagine that during the last few years no professional has equalled his record of earnings in the big tournaments for big prize money.

To-day he is obviously a thoughtful person with plenty of decided and rather original notions as to the playing of the game. I remember for example his telling me that when he taught Mrs Sarazen to play golf he insisted on her learning with heavy clubs. I am afraid to say how heavy they were; they sounded to me almost cruelly so, but they had the right effect in making the pupil swing the club and let it do the work. It is probably on this principle that he himself is apt to practise swinging not with one club but with two or even three (it is a baseball player's trick) so that he looks like a lictor with a whole bundle of rods; but then he is as strong as a little bull and could doubtless swing a bundle of battle axes.

Not only has he thought much about method but he is using his head all the time and plays the game strategically. At Prince's he several times took a spoon off the tee, so that he could reach the best place from which to play the second shot, without any fear of going just too far. It was particularly noticeable how he always took this spoon for his tee shot to the 15th. There was here no danger of the rough in going too far, but the pitch to that small plateau, cocked up amid all manner of perils, is perceptibly easier if it is not too short and so the ball can be hit the harder. How wise in him it was too to take his iron for the second at the 17th in the last round, when he was growing rather shaky and knew it. In the other rounds he had been hitting the most glorious seconds right home with wood, but this time his ball lay a little more to the right, the danger of the bunker was a little greater and his confidence was a little on the wane; so he took his iron and played safely for a five. It is not everyone who would have had so much self-control at that moment, for the strokes had been slipping away, he knew all about Havers's 68 and, in short, things were not too comfortable.

That grin of his is the mark of a sunny and delightful nature, but not of an altogether placid one. He has had, unless I am much mistaken, to overcome something in his Latin blood that used to surge up untimely. Like Bobby Jones, he can boil inside and sometimes on rare occasions he used to boil over. When he was second to Hagen in the Open championship at Sandwich in 1928 he might have won or at least have tied but for one little ebullition. It was at the Suez Canal hole; his ball lay in the rough off the tee and his admirable caddie wanted him, I feel pretty sure, to take an iron. He took wood, missed the shot badly and then advanced on the ball again with the same club without giving himself time to think. Just for that moment he lost himself and that disastrous hole may well have lost him the championship. He would not have done that at Carnoustie last year when he fought on with a fine stoicism in the face of adverse fate. Twice in the course of the three days the wind changed between morning and afternoon, and each time it changed in favour of Armour and against Sarazen. That, to be sure, is one of those things that are 'all about the game' but it made a great difference. Sarazen's only comment was that in order to win 'you must have the breaks' – an undeniable truth but one hard to enunciate calmly in times of disappointment.

At Prince's he had no 'breaks' as far as the play or the weather

37

were concerned. Indeed, in one respect he seemed rather unlucky, for he constantly hit the hole with his putts and the ball did not drop; but this misfortune is perhaps inherent in his method; he goes boldly for the back of the tin and will have no truck with timorous trickling in at the side door. One bit of luck he did have in that he was drawn to start early on the last day, and so he could, just as in his original triumph at Skokie, set up a mark for his wretched pursuers to shoot at. He left Havers with a 68 to tie, and that was a task that seemed hopeless. I should have written 'was' instead of 'seemed' had it not been for Sarazen's own achievement in the American championship a fortnight later. Then he was left with a 69 to tie. He did a 66 and won by three strokes. If anybody likes to say that this was, in the circumstances, the greatest round of golf ever played, I do not see how anybody else can quarrel with him.

Finally in our Open champion we salute not merely one of the finest hitters of a golf ball that ever lived but also one worthy of the name of a good golfer, than which no man can look forward to a better epitaph. We may apply to him Hazlitt's famous words about Cavanagh the fives player, and I shall write them down yet again just for the pleasure of doing so. 'He had no affectation, no trifling. He did not throw away the game to show off an attitude, or try an experiment. He was a fine, sensible, manly player, who did what he could'. Of that last round at Fresh Meadow at any rate we may add Hazlitt's final sentence – 'but that was more than anyone else could even affect to do'.

A Long Flog Home (1935)

It is a hard world and Deal is in particular a hard course for those who cannot hit the ball far enough. Shortness is of course relative and I do not propose to define in terms of yards a short driver. All I say is that many a player who on other courses can perhaps blind himself to the fact that he is not very long has this delusion ruthlessly ripped from him when he plays at Deal from the back tees. He may fare tolerably well going out, but when he has his nose turned for the long flog homeward, and especially when he comes to that tremendous finish of four holes against the wind, then he must see himself for what he is – a puny creature. On the course where he usually plays he may find that he has to take a brassie in order to get up with his second where lustier folk take irons, and that is hard work; but at Deal he finds that he cannot reach the green at all. That is a bitter revelation in point of self-satisfaction and an expensive one in point of holes.

'Poor old So-and-So is dreadfully short,' is a remark very often heard there from the thoughtless lips of youth, after the ball has been dispatched down the course what used to be deemed a more than creditable distance, and two poor old So-and-So's in double harness, each a little stiff in the back, each unable to make the club whistle through the air as they once used, have a cheerless time of it. Delightful things may happen; they may hole putts; their longer-driving enemies may go into bunkers; but it is idle to deny that the dice are loaded against them.

I am saying these things neither in praise of mere hitting nor by way of whimpering complaint. On the contrary, I have an immense respect for that home-coming at Deal, which I deem magnificent, even though it be too magnificent for such as me. I have likewise a great respect for those who can hit the ball far, especially with their brassies. They deserve their reward, and let it always be remembered that long hitting does not come merely from strength, but from swinging the club in the right way. I am only pointing out that at Deal in particular they do get their reward in rich measure. Full justice is not always done nor full scope given to the man who can hit a long, high, carrying second over a cross bunker and make the ball stop on the green beyond. It is sometimes implied that the modern ball goes so far and the modern clubs are so good that anyone can reach the holes; it is even said, though only by very resolute old fogeys, that golf has lost the athletic quality that once belonged to it. I fancy that no-one would say so who has watched golf in the Halford-Hewitt Cup. Never was better illustrated the cruel truth that the ball 'maun be hit'.

It would surely be superfluous to preach a sermon on the text that long driving must also be straight driving. Of course it must, and the architect of today is rightly determined that as far as in him lies he will enforce the long driver's duty not merely of being accurate but of taking risks in order to reap the full benefit of his powers. Very long straight driving will always, and quite properly, be an immense asset, especially in match play. No one likes to be outdriven, and everyone must sympathise with that admirable golfer at Deal who, after playing as a substitute and doing great deeds, thanked Heaven that at last he had found someone he could outdrive. He had almost come to regard himself as the 'one poor tiger who had not got a Christian'.

Armour Takes the Breaks (1931)

There is some judgement but a great deal of luck in seeing the important things at an Open championship, and it was wholly luck that made me see the most crucial of all incidents in Armour's last and victorious round at Carnoustie.

There is one point on the links where everyone forgathers. It is close to the ominous wood of black firs into which luckless people may hook the ball at the short 8th hole. Here the 7th, 8th, 12th and 13th holes all more or less converge, and here I was standing on the last afternoon, rather dizzy in the midst of a whirlpool of rumours. Along came Armour to the 12th hole and hit a magnificent brassie shot right onto the middle of the 12th green, which very few players could reach in two. Rumour, which turned out for once not to be lying, said that his score was two under fours. That was just about good enough to win, even though he had started five shots behind Jurado, and clearly he must be watched.

He struck his long putt perfectly and the ball slipped past the edge of the hole not more than two feet away. Then he took rather a long while and missed the two-foot putt by a good two inches. To the next, the short 13th, he played a poor tee-shot and the ball ended off the green, rather fortunately not in heather or sand. Armour came up to play his chip and it was clear that his emotions had almost beaten him. He waggled and he looked up at the hole with a quick turn of the head, and he went on waggling and looking until no-one else could bear to look at him. If he misses this one, I thought to myself, he is done; but he waited until he could settle down, he laid it nearly dead and he holed the putt. The crisis was past and he went on playing lovely golf to the end.

In the evening I told him that I had seen those two holes, and he agreed that they had settled the issue. No-one could believe, he said, what a blow that short putt missed had been; there he was playing beautifully and then came this sudden, staggering shock. If, he added, his tee-shot to the 13th had found trouble, as it well might, he was 'gone', and, even when it did not, he felt he simply could not play the next shot because his brain was whirling like a mill-race, and he was thinking and thinking about everything in the whole world except the business in hand. Our Open championship was the one thing he wanted to win, and he felt himself on the verge of throwing it all away.

One could almost see him thinking all these things, and I have told the story at length both because I hope it is rather interesting and because it shows the kind of golfer that the new champion is. He is full of imagination, a bundle of quivering nerves kept fiercely under control, and this is the kind of temperament that either breaks a player of games or makes him terribly formidable. As a striker of the ball, except sometimes when it is dead at the holeside, Armour is truly magnificent. I do not believe that Taylor or Vardon at their best ever gave themselves so many possible putts for three with their iron shots as he does, and his style is the perfection of rhythm and beauty. From the beginning of the week I bored all our small party at the hotel by telling them that Armour was the best player in the field, and I am not likely to recant now.

A man may be the best player and still he cannot win the championship unless the luck be with him. Armour unquestionably had the luck of the weather, and at the end of the first two days he said that, having had the luck, he had missed the chance of getting away with a substantial lead. The wind blew pretty hard on Wednesday morning and Thursday afternoon. It lulled on

Wednesday afternoon and Thursday morning. Sarazen and Farrell had to play their first round on Wednesday morning and their second on Thursday morning; Armour and Jurado had to do exactly the opposite, and while their advantage cannot be exactly computed in strokes it was a very real one. Had matters been the other way round, either Sarazen or Farrell might have won. As Gene said, 'You have to take the breaks', and they did not have them.

The last three holes at Carnoustie with the wind blowing from the east (which is not the normal way or the best way for the course) make up just about the most testing and perilous finish in all golf. Consequently there were several tragedies enacted there. If Alliss could have done the last two in four and five he would have tied with Armour's score, and he took five and six with a dreadfully superflous shot out of bounds at the last. Then there was MacDonald Smith. This was the supreme effort of a golfing lifetime on his own native heath; he had pulled round splendidly from a bad start in his first round and he was playing like clockwork in his last. He wanted 3, 4, 5, par golf, to beat Armour, and could afford to lose one stroke and yet tie with him. He lost four strokes in two holes and finished 5, 6, 5. I saw the six at the 17th, without his ball touching any form of hazard, and I felt rather as if I had gone to see a man hanged. Finally, and most poignant of all, was Jurado's tragedy, also at the 17th. He wanted a four and a five to win, and it seemed as if he could hardly fail to get the two fives to tie, for the 17th down the wind, though not an easy four, is quite an easy five. One thought of all sorts of mistakes he might make but one never dreamed of the one he did make, when he popped the ball into the burn off the tee, more or less in front of his nose. It was terribly sad, for he is a splendid little man (he does not weigh 10 stone) and had played splendidly courageous golf, full of smiling excitement but always keeping control of himself. I wish these horrid things were not inevitable in championships.

Yet another tragedy, of course, had happened earlier in the day, and that was the breakdown of Cotton in his third round, when

British hopes of his winning were very high. Cotton today is a great golfer, and I think his time will surely come but a championship only comes once a year, and he that will not when he may, etc. The technical cause of his downfall was, as it seemed to me, that he was getting on the wrong side of the hole; he was sparing his approaches down the wind going out with the result that he left himself long down-wind putts. Continually to lay these dead is desperate work; he left himself too much to do, and when the ensuing five-foot putts went astray his game began to disintegrate. No doubt there was a more general cause, too, namely, that though Cotton has tried hard to school a naturally rebellious temperament, he has not yet wholly succeeded, and when things went wrong he could not quite stand the strain. It is this control that he has to practise now, for his hitting of the ball is just about good enough for anything or anybody.

Hydes and Jekylls (1935)

Every golfer has a dual nature, in every one of us a Jekyll and a Hyde are constantly contending. The Jekyll of the story was a fine, well-grown man, while Hyde was light and dwarfish. Of most golfers I am afraid that the converse is much more nearly true: Jekyll is small, sickly, puny; Hyde a lusty monster. Yet even the worst of us have our moments, not in which we are wholly virtuous, but in which the good for all too short a while conquers the evil. It is then that we display the temperate smoothness, the suavity and rhythm of a Jekyll, that all unseemly haste and passion are temporarily absent from our swing, that we stand up to the ball as though we feared to look no man in the face. And then there comes over us swiftly the dreadful change, and it is our own doing. Sometimes we have, like that unhappy doctor, 'smarted in the fires of abstinence' too long, so that there catches us by the throat a sudden lust to hit the ball hard, as hard as ever we can. At others we 'lick the chops of memory', contrasting with our present and insipid methods the gorgeous carefree driving of some unforgettable summer evening, when it did not seem to matter how we stood or how quickly we swung or even whether we looked at the ball.

Again it may happen that we do not fall through any active wickedness, but suffer only, as did Dr Jekyll at the outset of his career, from 'a certain impatient gaiety of disposition'. We want some new and comparatively innocent experience; we grow

tired, however modestly successful it may be, of our own style
and think it would be amusing to imitate somebody else's or to
try only for a stroke or two insidious advice that we have read in
a book. It matters not precisely how our fall is accomplished; we
ourselves have precipitated it, and our devil, long caged, comes
out roaring.

All too easily can we recognise the marks of change. The Hyde
in us is unmistakable. Observe his tense muscles, his evil crouch,
his furious address to the ball, his reckless loss of balance, his ape-
like contortions. For a moment or two we find a hideous enjoyment in his antics, we leap at the ball with a misbegotten confidence, but too soon the spirit of hell awakes in us and we lash and
slash till, on a sudden, tragedy and destruction overtake us. Then
realising our danger, even as Hyde did after battering Sir
Dancers Carew to death, we fly back to Jekyll as our city of
refuge, only to find that we are cut off from it, that we have not
got the key.

It will be remembered that the magic draught failed at last; the
reconversion from Hyde to Jekyll no longer took place. Its
inventor believed that this was owing to some quality in one of
the original ingredients which was absent from all the fresh
supplies for which he ransacked the chemists' shops in London.
Whether this was really so or whether the elixir had lost its
potency from some subtler reason we cannot tell. It matters not
which it was; our case is that of Dr Jekyll. We can recall, in its
minutest details as to hips or elbows, the remedy which has
before transmuted us from a pressing, forcing demon to a
leisurely, true-swinging Christian. We can swear that we have
forgotten nothing; stance, grip, even waggle are precisely as they
were in happier days; we go through all the motions as we did
before – and nothing happens. There come none of the moment-
arily racking pains of change to end in an overpowering passion of
relief; Hyde is still in full possession. Nor can we ever tell whether
we have unconsciously varied the recipe or whether that particular potion has become stale and unprofitable.

I have been talking hitherto of the everyday run of sufferers.

There are some golfers so great, dwelling so far above us on such cold, chaste heights that it is hardly possible to believe of any one of them that he contains even a germ of Hyde. They may have been, as was Dr Jekyll, wild in their youth and, indeed, I have heard one of the most famous of golfers remark that he did not like to see a youngster too careful; but look at them now, stately, polished monuments of control! We cannot harbour even the breath of a suspicion. When we saw Harry Vardon swing the club (would that we could see him now!) we thought that here was not an impure Jekyll in which the good preponderated, but pure unsullied good, even as Hyde was pure evil. On the other hand, there are very, very great ones in whom the fiend lurks. Let me take as an example, with infinite respect, the sage of Walton Heath [James Braid]. Just once in a while, when he gives his club an additional waggle, when his knees crumple beneath him with the exuberance of the blow, when he hits a stupendous and magnificent hook into the heather, do we not catch a glimpse beneath that angelic exterior of the simian Hyde? And is there not, O my fellow sinners, just a grain of comfort in that?

Lovelock's Mile (1934)

There is no doubt where I ought to have been last Saturday; I ought to have been at Wentworth watching the match at golf between England and France. I shirked it unashamedly and went to watch something which I deemed, with all respect to the golfers, better worth the seeing, the mile race at the White City between Lovelock and Bonthron.

Nothing in this life, not even our next holiday, is ever quite so good as we think it is going to be, and, apart from the glorious circumstance that the right man won, I suppose that this great mile was just the least bit disappointing. Yet I would not have missed it for any earthly consideration. Why, the buzz of excitement when the men came out was alone worth all the money; one could have wished for a false start or two to prolong it. So of course was that supreme instant that comes in every race, when we could shout 'He's got him!' with defiant conviction, with no timid thought of propitiating the Fates. So most of all in this undemonstrative country was the genuinely emotional rush of dark and light blue blazers to embrace the victor.

Then, almost as good as any of these things in a less agitating way was the talk afterwards. I stood silent and awestricken among the heroes of old. There was one whose record had stood for seven-and-forty years and still stood at the end of the day, though it had a nasty shake; I swear I saw his jaw drop when the artist on the loud-speaker announced forty-eight and paused a second before coming to the four-fifths. There was another whose half-mile is immortal and I shook his revered hand. There was a third whom I had seen as a schoolboy when he won his first mile at Queen's Club, looking very prim and young with very large, round spectacles, and Oxford thought that they could beat him and found themselves deliciously wrong. There was, to mention just one more, he who I had seen nearly forty years ago rolling down the straight at the end of a famous quarter with a famous red head behind him. These, and 'such great men as these', had much to say of the tactics of the race. Ought the Cornell pace-maker to have gone faster for the first two laps? Why, when with Leach in close attendance he did draw some eight yards ahead, did Bonthron seem disinclined to go up and stayed behind with that pattering dark blue Nemesis at his heels? There was one there, a great ally of Cambridge and I think the shrewdest of them all, who when those first two laps were done foretold the end. The Americans, he said, were playing into Lovelock's hands, for if it was going to come to a finish, there was only one man who could win it.

What fun it all was! I could not help feeling that, exciting and agonising as golf can be, it lacks a little something in that element of tactics. Perhaps it would be more than we could endure if it had it, and we ought to be thankful. At any rate, say what we will, it does lack it. Golf is a contest of temperament, but not of wits. We may be tactical in playing short of a bunker or taking a particular line, but that is only with the view of doing the hole as well as we think we can, not in order to outwit or bamboozle the enemy. We cannot say to ourselves, 'All right, if he wants to do fives we will do fives too and come with a rush of fours at the end.' If we attempted any such insanity we should be far more likely to come with a rush of sixes. Even in a qualifying round in score play the golfer cannot save up his best efforts for the real test to come; he cannot keep the ball out of the hole if it wants to go in, although he knows that, against his will, he is using up the ration of putts which is all the grudging Fates allow a mortal. No; all we can do at golf is to play as well as we can from the very start and to the

49

very end. That is a very dull remark, perhaps, but it may be nearly the whole truth.

I remember a rather bombastic young gentleman, a very fine golfer, coming in much pleased with himself after the first round of a championship. He had been drawn against one who had beaten him in another tournament and he had had his revenge. 'I was determined to have no nonsense about it this time,' he proclaimed, 'I went all out from the very start,' and proceeded to reel off an imposing list of fours. 'That's all very well,' commented an eminent and long-suffering personage, 'but suppose he had gone all out from the start too.' The young gentleman was a little damped and could make no answer. Indeed there is no answer to make, for, as I said, there is nothing to do but to start as well as possible and keep it up as long as possible. A golfer is sometimes said to spurt and the word is permissible, for it conveys a picture, but his spurt is not like that of a runner, deliberately kept back waiting for the right moment. What, in fact, happened was that, having played badly, he began to play better; he would have liked to have done those fours and threes earlier in the round if he could and then he would not have needed them at the finish; there would not have been a finish because he would have been walking in triumphantly from the 14th green.

There are, to be sure, tactical methods of harassing the enemy, but our fellows do not think very well of us if we employ them. We must not walk fast if our opponent does not like being hurried – a method sometimes recommended by the older race of Scottish caddies; we must not lie on our stomachs interminably contemplating the line of the putt against one who is notoriously impatient of delay. We must not – perhaps most criminal of all – say that we should like to give our adversary a short putt but feel regretfully bound to see him hole it. There is something else in that matter of short putts which we ought not to do to him and yet I am sure we often do it, though not of malice aforethought. We concede with an airy grace a couple of short ones and then when he has a rather shorter one to tackle we stand silent, like graven images, contemplating the distant horizon. I have seen this highly effective course of conduct, but it is not a laudable one, and if we never gave short putts the question would not arise.

I heard the other day of a case of rather greater subtlety. B had two for it on the first green from a moderate distance and A at once gave him the hole. Said a friend to A: 'That was rather a lot to give. I should have let him putt.' A replied: 'He might have holed in one and that would have given him confidence in his putting.' Was this a permissible piece of tactics or was A rather too deep a dog? I am not prepared to give a verdict, but I am sure of this: that the oftener I am given the hole when I have two for it the better I shall be pleased.

Freedom to Skip (1952)

There may not be many advantages in being grown-up, but there is at any rate one; the Archbishop of York will not insist on our finishing a book once we have begun it, whether we like it or not. This, he says, is now and then very good discipline for a boy, but we who are older, need not continue the unequal struggle. There are various motives that can impel us to go on ploughing through a book long after we are bored. There is first of all what Thomas Hughes called 'the consciousness of silent endurance so dear to the heart of every Englishman', a quality which, in spite of his unquestioned greatness, he could sometimes himself evoke. Then there is the knowledge that the book is a classic and that it is the part of an educated man to have at least forgotten it. Memory recalls one, of a wide and admirable taste in literature, who observed 'I only finished *Joseph Andrews* by repeated charges at the point of the bayonet'. There is the desire, mild but insistent, to know what happens and who marries whom, or in the case of thrillers, and Dr Garbett expressly admits an occasional thriller, who did it. Two rather more particular reasons are that somebody has given us the book or the author is a friend of ours, so that in either case we must be prepared to withstand cross-examination.

To be made to read a book is some way towards loathing it. During Mr Wooster's brief engagement to Lady Florence Craye she made him read a book called *Types of Ethical Theory*, of which he remarked bitterly that doubtless it was all true but 'not the sort of thing to spring on a lad with a morning head'. Apart from so extreme a case, there are at least two dangers in the suggested compulsion. One is that it may implant in the young man's breast lasting hatred for a book which, had he begun it a year or so later, would have been his friend for life. The other, applicable both to boys and grown-ups, is that under any such hypothetical law nothing but short stories would be read and so, ultimately, written. The mere mass of pages would appal all but the bravest who would venture on *War and Peace*, and what a passion of pleasure many people would have lost by their cowardice! As to Sir Walter Scott, one glance at the first chapter would too often be enough. What is needed by one beginning, for example, *Ivanhoe* is that a kindly Archbishop should take the young reader by the hand and bid him never mind the Normans and Saxons, but start with Gurth and Wamba and 'The Curse of St Withold upon these infernal porkers!' Among all the freedoms which are today so peculiarly precious we must never forget freedom to skip.

Let the Better Side Lose (1937)

Which is the more enviable lot for the onlooker at a game – to care too much who wins or not to care at all?

At the present moment the problem is not a very acute one for the golfing spectator. There is a surcease during which he can rest his shattered nerves, but soon the spring will come and then his agony, if he is of the agonising kind, will begin again. That it can be an agony no one with any experience will deny. Indeed his case is the harder in that he cannot, as in some other game, gain relief in moments of tension from a prodigious roaring and bellowing. During all those long-drawn-out preparations for the crucial putt he can do no more than grip his neighbour by the shoulder, and can only greet its ultimate failure with a hollow and smothered groan. Many a time in watching the University match I have felt bitterly jealous of those who, having from their upbringing no predisposition in favour of either side, can look on with a detached and Olympian air, How offensively calm they are! With what a hatefully condescending smile do they view the contortions of us who are so cruelly interestє d! They are at pains to explain why young so-and-so got into a particular bunker, whereas to us the only point is that he did get in, and that this is either a shame and a calamity or a cause for dancing, not too overtly, a fandango of joy.

I must confess that I have seldom attained to this quintessence of impartiality. The match may be one in which I have no right or title to take sides, and yet sooner or later partisanship, as did cheerfulness in the case of Mr Edwards, will break through. Some gallant shot by one side, some tediousness of address on the part of the other, sets the spark to the ever-ready fuel of prejudice. Moreover, the vanity of the critic often supplements the rancour of the partisan. The observer may begin by not caring twopence for either A or B, but sooner or later he is sure to remark out of the profundity of his wisdom, 'That's settled it. B will go right away now, you'll see.' Once he has thus committed himself, he is naturally indignant if A insists on falsifying his prophecy by refusing to collapse. The thought becomes father to the wish, and B has got to win to save the spectator's face.

Yet the hope of being one day the perfectly impartial watcher of a game has never died within my breast, and last week it seemed for a while that I had attained it. Being at Brighton I went to watch a match at ice hockey between two illustrious teams, the Brighton Tigers and the Wembley Lions. I believed that my admiration and respect were equally divided between them, while the critic's vanity clearly could play no part; I had only seen this tremendous game once before in my life, when I had cheered, but with discretion, for the Harringay Racers. On opening my programme I was swayed this way and that. The name of Mr Romeo Patsy Sequin, the Tiger's goalminder, warmly engaged my sympathies, but that of Mr Jo-Jo Graboski, centre-ice for the Lions, was equally seductive and redressed the balance. When the teams appeared the Tigers looked worthy of their name in yellow and black stripes, but the red and white of the Lions were very agreeable too. My judgement was the cooler from the fact that, owing to the pathetic sneezing and snuffling of a destined companion, I had to go by myself, and so I sat there in that bedlam of shouters 'solitary as in the woods of Yucatan'.

There was a cheer-leader with a megaphone who led his supporters through various preliminary and complicated yells always ending in 'Tigers', and that is all I know, except that at first they almost persuaded me to be Lion. That was before the game began, and perhaps for the first ten minutes after it had begun I remained as austerely and impartially as I was ignorantly observant. It is, however, impossible to watch ice hockey without growing excited, and once you are excited you are lost; you must want somebody to win. Towards the end of the end of the first period something happened at the speed of thought; the red light blazed to show that the Tigers had scored, and, as an old nurse of naughty children used to say, 'all Pandora was let loose'. From that moment I became a naturalized Tiger. My intellect, if I may so term it, might glow with admiration of the great Mr Lou Bates as he flashed up the ice, splendid and seemingly irresistible, but my heart was once and for all with Mr Romeo Patsy Sequin (I really must write this name down again), who placidly deflected his shot. I was too self-conscious to shout with my neighbours 'Good old Bobby!' in praise of the dashing Mr Lee, but I should like to have done so, and when the last gong sounded I heaved a sigh of true relief. The Tigers – my Tigers – had won by three goals to one.

After this nerve-racking but delicious experience I shall never try to be impartial any more, being convinced once and for all that it is mistaken. It is better to have loved and lost than never to have loved the Tigers at all. What is more, I am prepared to love the Racers, the Royals, the Monarchs, the Hawks, or even the Lions at reasonable notice. Let us have no more nonsense about the better side winning! I am at the moment so thoroughly demoralised that I could almost cheer the missing of a putt.

The Jolly Dog Club (1941)

There came a notable couple who survived for years, Pat and Whisk. Pat was an Irish terrier, Whisk a Scottish one, or as he was then called, an Aberdeen. His name, when he was bought, had been Whisky, but this was unendurable and was shortened accordingly. They were sufficiently good friends in that both belonged to the same association – we called it the Jolly Dog Club – for investigating the dust-heaps on the Huntingdon road, but they were entirely unlike one another in character. Whisk was clever while Pat was undeniably stupid. With great difficulty and much against his will he learnt to give one paw, his left, and nothing in the world would make him give the other. Over and over again he would tender that one wistful, persistent paw, conscious that he was not at his best and was being made a fool of, but having a reasonable wish for water biscuit. Beyond that his dignity would not let him descend. Meanwhile, Whisk was like a small boy in class anxious to answer a question and holding up his hand 'in a restless agony of superior information'. He had a considerable number of accomplishments, the most engaging of which perhaps were the banging of his two sable paws on the table-cloth in 'Up Jenkins' and sitting in a little armchair, modelled I believe on one in Ely Cathedral, where he looked like a rather dissipated black bishop. He was dying with eagerness to go through his repertory and resented the time wasted by Pat's fumbling. He was exceedingly possessive over his dinner, and it was an unvarying tradition to ask him when in the middle of it whether it was good. To these questions he replied by the most ferocious growling with his mouth full.

Whisk was brilliant in a showy way and Pat was slow, reserved and infinitely faithful, with a touching simplicity of character, that would have melted a heart of stone. He was a one-man dog, for, though he was fond of us all, his real adoration was kept for my father. He seems to me in looking back rather like a certain type of regular soldier, with no very wide range of ideas, but a simple faith, a strong sense of duty, and indomitable courage. He would fight anything on four legs, and that, I am sure, he deemed part of his duty, since he all too easily snuffed insults to his family. All other dogs apparently said rude things about us, so that the challenge trembled perpetually on his lips. He had one fault, and that he knew perfectly well to be naughty, namely, the occasional killing of chickens. Of this, no beating nor tying the victim round his neck could wholly cure him. He was sincerely penitent if ever a dog was, and passed the evening in great depression, hardly capable of appreciating the first movement towards forgiveness; but ever and anon the demon in him, grown stronger by abstinence, would come out roaring and another chicken had to be paid for. Not only he but the whole household used temporarily to be plunged into sorrow over this shortcoming, for there was about him a really heartrending pathos. He had no arts of wheedling or insinuating; he did not mean to be pathetic; he only meant to be good and that made his sins the harder to bear. All dogs are touching, but Pat's delight, when a walk was in prospect, and his grin of affection, went terribly straight to the heart.

Some years ago there was an account in the newspapers of the 'Talking Dogs' of Mannheim. They were supposed to have learned to express themselves in a code by the beatings of their tails, and this new science was called typtology. It is, I suggest, a good thing that they have had no successors, for it is the muteness of the dog's appeal that gives it half its charm. If typtology had been widely taught in the days of Pat and Whisk, Whisk would doubtless have poured out an endless flood of gossip, largely egotistical, but partly also, since he was a great scavenger, on the entrancing odours in the neighbourhood. He would have talked us all down; but Pat, if he could ever have mastered the alphabet, would have said but little. A halting word or two of affection possibly, a desire for his game of ball assuredly – that is as far as he would have gone. His one supreme merit consisted in being a true gentleman to the very bottom of his soul.

My father had later another Aberdeen terrier, answering to the pleasant name of Scrubbins. He had belonged to a friend who died and, since he was then both homeless and mangy, his fate was almost sealed. However, a kind vet cured him and he survived several years, a dog of considerable character and a most faithful friend to my father. Once or twice my father took him to the University Library, left him outside and forgot him. Scrubbins quite unperturbed went to the nearest cab-stand, where he was well known, and took a hansom home. One little scene in which he figured comes back to me. My sister was being married in the forbidding precints of the Cambridge Registry Office and Scrubbins had been left at the door. We were all ranged in due order before the table and the proceedings had begun, when a deliberate pit-a-pat was heard in the passage. Somebody got up to shut the door but the Registrar hastily interposed; the marriage, it appeared, would not be legal unless it were open to all comers to attend. So Scrubbins pattered in and behaved with perfect discretion and decorum. He added a cheerful note to the rather grim ceremony, and if there had been a vestry we were all satisfied that he would have signed his name in it.

Mr Ouimet Makes History (1913)

'Oh, bother abroad, I've been there,' says the schoolboy in an old du Maurier picture in *Punch* and I am afraid his remark represents my own frame of mind. Though a deplorably stay-at-home person, not to be tempted out of my rut by Athens or Venice, I had always wanted, sometimes passionately, to see America. It was in 1913 that Vardon and Ray made the first of their golfing tours there, and I think Lord Northcliffe paid some or all of their expenses. At any rate he was greatly interested in their tour and so I was sent to write about the Open championship in which they would be playing, and also about the Amateur championship, and any other golf that came my way. Lord Northcliffe gave me two final words of advice: to beware of drinking too much iced water and never to talk of America but always of the United States. Feeling at once much excited and a little forlorn and homesick I set out by myself in the *Baltic* at the end of August.

Odd little things remain with one from the first day in a new and memorable place, and I must put them down in a jumble just as they come, hoping that they are not too trivial or too dull. I had got for myself a room at the hotel at Garden City where the Amateur championship was to be played. Otherwise I did not know precisely what was going to befall me, and felt rather lonely and frightened as the ship came into New York. I was, however, soon to know what American hospitality could be. My friend, Mr Max Behr was then the editor of the American *Golf*

Illustrated, for which I wrote. I had never met him, though I had corresponded with him; he lived some twenty miles away, and my boat got in at about eight o'clock in the morning. Nevertheless, he got up at some unearthly hour to welcome me when I landed. I never was more grateful for anything in my life and I still think it was one of the kindest deeds I ever heard of.

The things that remain in my memory from that first day or two, though very pleasant to recall, are not of earthshaking importance. First of all there was the sight of the golf course at Garden City dotted with players in white flannels, like so many cricketers, or, stranger still, in shirt sleeves and knickerbockers. This may now have a prehistoric sound. Twenty-seven years ago we knew that Americans played, very wisely, coatless, and had even seen them do it on occasion. We had for instance seen Chick Evans at Prestwick in 1911. After struggling a whole round in a Norfolk jacket in a noble if misguided effort to spare our feelings, he had taken it off on the 19th green, alas! too late. Still a whole field of these, as they seemed, half-naked players was, however much one was prepared for it, a surprise.

Almost the first player I saw was Mr Jerome Travers, the reigning champion, whom I had met before in Scotland. He was just holing out at the last hole and a spectator asked him how he had fared. His answer was, 'About eighty, I guess,' and that stuck in my memory. Any British player in such a case would have said that he had played rather badly, or words to that vague effect (80 was not a great score at Garden City), or that he had lost by such and such a margin; but the American player always knows what his score has been: he will tell you what it was and leave you to draw your own conclusions. To the British this intense interest in the score is sometimes a little tiresome, and it certainly involves some superfluous holing out; but that it is good discipline for the soul can hardly be doubted; it prevents the player from getting slack and always gives him something to aim at.

I cannot remember whether it was on that first day or on the next that I was taken to spend the evening at Coney Island. I will not describe that famous resort except to say that it is like Earl's

Court set by the sea and multiplied almost to infinity. The switchbacks and scenic railways were altogether on a steeper and more magnificent scale than any I had seen. This fact I learned in a painfully practical manner, for not adhering quite carefully enough to my seat on the switchback, I came down with so fierce a bump as to sit with some discomfort during the rest of my stay in America. We bathed in the sea and had clams for dinner and amused ourselves very much. One of the party was a young gentleman called Francis Ouimet, who had just won the Massachusetts championship. Till that victory, I gathered, nobody had heard much of him, at least outside his native state, and he was still unknown to the general mass of golfers: he was a very pleasant young gentleman and enjoyed the switchbacks wholeheartedly, and I never thought that within less than a month he was destined to make an epoch in golf.

He began by doing a very good round in the qualifying competition, being one stroke ahead of Mr Walter Travis, and people began to wonder whether he could stand the strain of another round. He did stand it, and beat Mr Travis by a stroke only, as it turned out, to be ousted from first place by a wonderful last nine holes by Mr Chick Evans.

Then, in the second round of the match-play, he was drawn against Mr Jerome Travers. It was a great match, marked by some very fine golf, and Mr Travers won in the end by 3 and 2. Mr Ouimet drove very straight and easily, but hardly seemed quite long enough, for Mr Travers, using his fearful bludgeon of a driving iron, had something the best of matters from the tee. Mr Ouimet appeared a good putter with a nice smooth way of hitting the ball upon the green, but against Mr Travers he missed three very short putts, two of them at particularly important crises of the game. His iron play was accurate but appeared a little too loose, lacking something in firmness. Altogether he seemed an admirable player, full of great promise, but nobody expected him fully to 'arrive' for a year or two. When he got older and stronger, people said, he might do great things.

The victory of Mr Travers in that championship was in many

ways the most remarkable I ever saw. Here was a man who dare not use a wooden club from the tee and lived in constant dread of hitting his pitches off the socket; and yet he won and won easily, having only been at all closely pressed in a single match when he beat Ouimet. It was an astonishing feat, only possible for a player of indomitable, imperturbable temperament and a truly magnificent putter. Almost every day he went out, duly practising with that errant mashie which would periodically hit the ball towards cover-point, and I think by the end of the week he had more or less conquered the socketing. Yet he must have felt like the man in the ancient story whose opponent had the right to shout 'Boo' once in the round and won by constantly creeping up as if about to say it. It is not the shots we do socket that lose us the match but those we think we are going to socket. As for his driving from the tee with an iron, it was extremely long and straight but it did not satisfy his aesthetic longings. As soon as ever he was a hole or so up, he gallantly brought out his driver. The result was a frightful hook or two and the loss of his lead and so doggedly, and with a willing smile, he went back to his iron again. Only a player of rare placidity and powers of concentration could thus have rung the changes without being disturbed.

A fortnight after that match with Mr Travers, Mr Ouimet had not only done the great things prophesied for him, but much greater ones still. The Country Club at Brookline near Boston where the Open championship was played is so called because it is the oldest in America and justly proud of the fact. It is a very pretty spot and the course is good and picturesque with valleys and wooded hills and rocky promontories in one or two places. If it is not a 'big' course, it is yet a very sound one and quite difficult enough for any reasonable being. On this particular occasion it was rather a wet one because the weather broke down and behaved abominably. It rained and it rained and a damp raw mist hung about the trees.

I am not certain about the qualifying rounds, but it seems to me now to have rained throughout the championship proper and the day of the historic playing off of the tie was as horrid a one as could be. Vardon and Ray were naturally the centres of interest. They were, I think I may say, just a little bit better then than any American player. I had boldly said this to some American friends who asked the very natural question, 'Why are they better?' I could only answer that when they saw the players they would see what I meant, and when they did see Vardon and Ray they were so kind and forgiving to my arrogance as to say that I had been right. A solitary British spectator was naturally anxious that his champions should quit themselves well, and on the first day they did play well. There they were at the top of the tree and one or other of them ought to have won, but I think that on the last day they both fell to some extent victims to that feeling of loneliness, of being the few against the many, which is always liable to attack visiting players. Nobody who has not tried it knows how hard it is to play your best in the other man's country. The final rounds of 79 by Vardon and Ray were emphatically not worthy of the two great golfers who played them; they had recovered their courage finely, but they had made far too many bad shots. They seemed almost certain to be caught, and they deserved to be caught.

Suddenly, Ouimet was upon us, coming along to the 15th hole, which is close to the club-house. He had made a great recovery, but even so, when he had holed out at that 15th, he had to do the next three holes in ten shots to tie and the par figures for those three were 3, 4, 4. He got his three comfortably enough, but now he had to save a stroke somewhere, and each of the last two holes is a good four. He played two wellnigh perfect shots to the 17th, but still he was left with a downhill, curling putt. How long was it, that historic putt? In a cutting from my own description, I read that it was three yards and I hardly think that does the player justice. In an account by Mr Travers I read that it was 'twenty feet', and that I should say makes it too long. Perhaps it was somewhere between these two estimates. At any rate it was a putt that hardly seemed holeable at such a crisis and down it went, the ball taking the slope to perfection. Then there broke out such a tumult of cheers and yells and cat-calls as I never heard before or since.

I remember Lord Trevethin once telling how, being at the time the Judge of Assize, he went to see the match between Wales and New Zealand at Cardiff. When the great Teddy Morgan scored the most famous of all tries, he looked at the eminent citizens of Cardiff around him in the stand, their mouths wide open, their eyes darting out of their head, their hats thrown into the air, and he thought that they looked, one and all, like madmen. I recalled his words when Mr Ouimet holed that putt. All the most venerable of Bostonians appeared to have gone simultaneously mad, and for that matter, though my cheers were more restrained, I did not feel wholly sane myself.

The pandemonium soon died down, however, for the last hole still remained. Mr Ouimet played two fine shots, but his second did not clear the cross-bunker by much and the ball sat obstinately down on the muddy ground. His run up was a beauty, and still he was a couple of yards from the hole and then down went that putt too, and it was struck as if no other ending was possible. The clearest picture that remains to me is of the youthful hero playing all those last crucial shots, just as if he had been playing an ordinary game. He did not hurry; he did not linger: there was a briskness and decisiveness about every movement, and whatever he may have felt, he did not betray it by as much as the movement of an eyelash. Yet he did not play as one in a dream, as people sometimes do at supreme crises: he was just entirely calm and entirely natural.

It is hard to recollect what one thought before an event which happened some while ago, but, as far as I remember, I had no real doubt that Vardon and Ray would beat their young adversary next day. I felt fairly sure that they would win; I felt still more sure that, whatever they did, the real hero of the championship must be Mr Ouimet. I did not believe in the possibility of an actual defeat, but I felt that England had suffered a moral one. And if I had no very real fears, I think that the Americans had no real hopes. That their boy hero, after a night to sleep on it, should go out in cold blood and beat, not one, but two champions, was too much to hope for.

The day of the play off was damp and horrible. The ground was a sop. The players took towels with them to keep the handles of their clubs dry. But nothing could stop the crowd pouring out of Boston, and megaphones shouted them into their places. I had the honour assigned me of being Mr Ouimet's marker. It was a very pleasant one and also a very convenient one, for I could thus cling to the players and see everything. I cannot remember exactly when I began to feel thoroughly uneasy about the Englishmen's chances, but it was fairly soon. Mr Ouimet was so obviously master of himself and never looked like breaking down. He was driving right up to his competitors; he was doing everything as well as they could do it, and he was a better putter than either of them. There were just two moments when, if the young player meant to break down, he might have done so; the more serious of these was at the 5th.

It is a difficult two-shot hole with an out-of-bounds wood on the right-hand side. Into that wood Mr Ouimet sliced his second. Suppose after that disaster he should play another poor shot and take at least a six and possibly even a seven, and suppose that Ray and Vardon should get their fours, that might be the beginning of the end. In fact Mr Ouimet dropped another ball, hit a really glorious shot and got his five. The other two did not quite get home, and took five apiece. The shot out of bounds had cost nothing, a mistake had been grandly atoned for on one side, there had been disappointment and a chance lost on the other. After that, whatever happened, it was going to be a fight to the death. Of that one felt almost certain.

The play was so good, the strain so great, that someone was almost bound to bend under it, and at the 15th Ray was gone. Vardon remained, one stroke behind with three to play. The pair holed the 16th in three and then came the final blow. Vardon, realising I suppose that desperate measures were necessary, tried a short cut by means of a long carry. He just failed and took five. The longest way round proved the shortest way home. Mr Ouimet drove well out to the right, a beautiful second, and then, just as he had done before, holed the putt for three. Again all the world went justifiably mad. Only Mr Ouimet mattered now; nothing but a stroke of apoplexy could stop him and never did anyone look less apoplectic. There was a gruesome wait before his second shot, a long shot over a cross-bunker, sodden with the wet; the megaphone blared, the crowd marshalled itself, Mr Ouimet had one practice swing, then away soared the ball; it was a perfect long iron shot: from the moment it left the club it was a winning stroke. He got his four easily and with it his 72, and was swallowed up in the crowd. Vardon was round in 77, Ray in 78.

The next thing I remember is sitting in my bedroom looking out on the rain and writing frantically. I felt like a War Correspondent on some stricken field, sending home news of the annihilation of the British Army. But the victory had been so glorious that no grudging of it was possible. Next day I lunched with the young conqueror in the club-house, when he tranquilly consumed 'horse's neck', a pleasing drink, having nothing more exciting than lemon in it, and was the most unmoved of the party. Meanwhile outside the gates of The Country Club the Sunday papers poured out tempestuous columns and all America rang with his victory.

Mr Ouimet's play at Brookline was a revelation after Garden City. For one thing his driving had lengthened out in an amazing way. I believe that at Garden City, where the fairway is very narrow and length of no vast importance, he had been playing with rather a short, light club in order to ensure accuracy; but even so, no one could have anticipated such an exhibition of driving as he gave. With wet, heavy ground, and no sun to help him, he fully held his own with both Ray and Vardon from the tee. When Ray produced one of his most stupendous hits he was a little ahead; but on the whole, taking the whole match through, I think Mr Ouimet was the longest of the three, and certainly no one could have been straighter, because he only hit one single tee shot anywhere except down the exact centre of the course. In his iron play he seemed to have got perceptibly firmer and crisper, laying shot after shot close to the hole in the most approved professional manner, and as to his putting, he never looked in the least likely to miss a short one. The slight tendency to push the ball out to the right of the hole had, for the time at least, quite disappeared. To see a golfer improve so quickly in the course of a fortnight was, as I imagine it, like watching the mango tree grow up by the conjurer's art.

How good Mr Ouimet would be in a high wind it is impossible to say. He has, like most Americans, had little experience of golf in a wind. Possibly for a while it might trouble him, but he hits the ball so truly, and is so obviously fine a golfer that, no doubt, he would master the art quickly. If he comes over to England next year I do not think that we shall be able to rely on the wind to defend us. Sandwich, as far as I can judge, should suit his game particularly well, better perhaps than it will suit that of Mr Travers.

One of the pleasantest and most picturesque features of Mr Ouimet's victory was the appearance of his small caddie. How old he was I do not know, but he had considerable difficulty in keeping his employer's bag of clubs from trailing on the ground. Mr Ouimet for the most part held him by the arm and helped him to edge his small way through the crowd. When it came to the last hole, where there is a steep rise before the green, the poor little imp stuck altogether, and had to be almost carried over the crest. He was a most heroic child, and as cool as his master, bearing all the excitement at any rate with outward calm. He had carried for Mr Ouimet all through the tournament, and when it came to the final fight, someone tried, I believe, by an offer of some dollars to be allowed to take his place; but he stuck firmly to his post and was not to be seduced. When all was over a band of admirers made up a purse for him, and he went home laden with more dollars than he had ever before possessed.

Eternal Browsing (1941)

Reviewers are apt to say of a detective story that 'it is impossible to lay it down till the last page is reached'. It is rather for books of reference that such praise should be reserved. No others are comparable with them for the purposes of eternal browsing. They suggest all manner of lovely, lazy things, in particular the watching of a cricket match on a sunshiny day. We have only dropped in for half-an-hour, but the temptation to see just one more over before we go is irresistible. Evening draws on, the shadows of the fielders lengthen on the grass, nothing much is happening, a draw becomes every minute more inevitable, and still we cannot tear ourselves away. So it is with works of reference, even with the most arid, even with Bradshaw, whose vocabulary, as Sherlock Holmes remarked, is 'nervous and terse but limited'. Over the very next page of Bradshaw there may be hidden a Framlingham Admiral; adventure may always be in wait a little farther down the line. So, but a thousand times more so, is some exciting treasure trove awaiting us over the next page of this dictionary. [*The Oxford Dictionary of Quotations.*] What it is we cannot guess, but it is for ever calling in our ears to turn over just one more. We have only taken down the book to look up one special passage, but it is likely enough that we shall never get so far. Long before we have reached the appropriate letter we shall have been waylaid by an earlier one, and shall have clean forgotten our original quest. Nor is this all, for, if our mood changes as we browse, it is so fatally beautifully easy to change our pasture. We can play a game akin to that 'dabbing' cricket, so popular in private-school days, in which the batsman's destiny depended or was supposed to depend – for we were not always honest – on a pencil delivered with eyes tightly shut. We can close the book and open it again at random, sure of something that will set us off again on a fresh and enchanting voyage of not too strenuous discovery. Under this enchantment I have fallen deep. I have pored over the proofs so that only by a supreme effort of will could I lay them down and embark on the impertinent task of trying to write about them. I now send them back to their home with a sense of privation and loneliness. Here seems to me a great book. Then

'Deem it not all a too presumptuous folly'

this humble tribute to Oxford from another establishment across the way.

The Evening Round (1935)

A correspondent has just written to me saying that the time has surely come for me to dilate upon golf after tea. He even goes so far as to say that I ought to do it every year, and here, being painfully conscious of my own bad habits, I thought at first that I detected a rather bitter irony. On re-reading his letter I came to the conclusion that he meant kindly; the irony is to be found in the circumstance, which he did not know, that I am not allowed to play golf even before tea.

The supreme moment can only come once a year, and this year I have missed it. For certain people it always comes on the same day, the Saturday of a weekend at Worlington. Then when the serious business of the day is over we sally forth with one club apiece. No doubt other and happier people did so last Saturday, but I had gone home snuffling and sneezing to bed, and that particular moment cannot be recaptured till another whole year has passed. Even as I write some time after tea there is plenty of light in the garden, light for putting and pitching, light even for what I am pleased to call driving, but it may not be.

The case, it may be said, is not a very hard one; the time of the first green mist on the hedges, of the first cuckoo that is not a mischievous little boy, has not yet come; there are plenty of evenings ahead. Yet the maddening part of golf is that the only time we feel a real longing to play it is when we cannot do so. In the morning I was allowed out for a little walk in the fresh air. I was exceedingly well wrapped up, and felt like Uncle Joseph in the coat of marten's fur and the health boots prescribed by Sir Faraday Bond. All Nature seemed determined to emphasise my lamentable state. In a little wood a missel-thrush sang loudly and triumphantly, and if ever a thrush sang 'Golf after tea' that was the identical bird.

Through the wood there runs a wide, grassy glade. It was all flecked with sunshine and had in it just a suspicion of a 'dog-leg' bend to the right, that kept calling and calling in my ears for a shot with a little drift in it. I plodded to the end of it – the prescribed limit of my walk – and turned; there was an equally fascinating bend to the left, and it positively shouted, 'Now for a little hook!' Outside the wood lay a meadow, bathed in light, close-cropped and inviting, with not so much as a single intrusive cow in it. All the new styles that I had thought of as I lay in my bed came welling up simultaneously in my mind and I could not try a single one of them, because it would never do to get 'overheated'. I was assured that I should be able to do it another day, but I did not want to do it another day; I may never want to do it on any other day, but I did so dreadfully want to have just one shot then.

There is something magical about the first rounds of spring, so that we remember some of them long, long after we have played them, not on account of any petty personal triumphs or disasters, but from the pure joy of being alive, club in hand. There was one Easter half at school, when the sun was so hot and the ground so dry that I lay and basked on the grass between my shots. I can see the particular spot now, just after turning away from the river and the terrific short hole with the solitary willow behind the green. There was another round at Sandwich, a first round on that noble course before a first University match. There was no lying on the grass that time, but a rush straight from the station to the club-house, and a race round the course in a blue serge suit to beat the fading daylight. Yet the same kind of ecstatic glory hangs round the memories of both rounds; I know that in the first of them my driver had a brown head, and in the second a yellow one, or perhaps, since the occasion was so romantic, I should say, of palest gold.

By way of encouraging in myself this maudlin state of mind I have been looking in an ancient diary to see which day of the year, something over thirty years ago, saw the first evening round. As a rule it was year in and year out within a day or two of this very Saturday, March 9, but in one year it came much earlier. On one February 25 I find recorded a tremendous display of energy; first of all a 36-hole Single, won at the very last hole, and then 'Played a 14-hole match afterwards which lost'. Since no margin is given I think it may safely be stated that it was lost by a good many holes. What time of the morning we started and why we did it I cannot state; indeed if I did not know myself to have kept that diary with remarkable honesty I should not believe in the entry any more than I believe in those gentlemen who are incapable of deception and write to the newspapers to say thàt they have heard the cuckoo in February.

The time of third rounds is over and will not come back. It is pitch dark outside my window now, but the daylight will come back and perhaps, if it is very warm and sunshiny, I shall be let out, without that confounded muffler, for just one spring shot with my springy driver. I wonder which style I shall try.

The Best-Known Figure in England (1934)

If one had to choose a single epithet to describe him, it would, I think, be simple. He did not think very deeply or very subtly about anybody or anything; perhaps not even about cricket, although his knowledge of it was intuitively profound, his judgement of a cricketer unique. His interests were all of the open air. If people wanted to read books, no doubt they got pleasure from it, but it was a pleasure that he could not really understand. Wisden, yes, perhaps, to confirm a memory or refute an argument, or in winter as an earnest of the summer to come; but in a general way books were bad for cricket. 'How can you expect to make runs,' he said to one of the Gloucestershire side, 'when you are always reading?'; and added, almost gratuitously, 'You don't catch me that way.' I have searched in vain for anyone who ever saw him take the risk, except in the case of a newspaper or a medical book in which he wanted to look up a point.

W. G. was not an intellectual man, and even as regards his own subject his was not an analytical brain, but by instinct or genius – call it what you will – he could form a judgement of a cricketer to which all others bowed. A schoolboy who had made innumerable runs for his school, and was generally regarded as an extraordinary cricketer, played in his first first-class match with W. G., and made a respectable score. Everybody crowded round the oracle to hear the verdict and expected a favourable one. 'He'll never make a first-class cricketer' – that was all, and it turned out to be entirely true. Here is a converse example. When Mr Jessop first appeared for Gloucestershire, those who now realise that they ought to have known better were struck only by the more rough-hewn and bucolic aspects of his batting. 'What have you got here, old man?' they asked W. G. rather disparagingly. 'Ah, you wait and see what I've got here,' he answered with a touch of truculence, and went on to say that in a year or so this would be the finest hitter that had ever been seen. That this verdict also turned out true is hardly worth saying.

He had that sort of quickness of apprehension that may, without disrespect, perhaps be called cunning, and is often to be found, a little surprisingly, in those who seem at first sight simple-minded and almost rustic. He had plenty of shrewdness too in judging the qualities of men, so far as they interested him and came within his sphere. He might occasionally do ill-judged things in the excitement of the moment, but at the bottom of everything there was a good hard kernel of common-sense.

We are told that when W. G. first appeared in first-class cricket he was shy, and we can picture him a tall, gawky, uneasy boy. He had not been to a public school; he came from a small country doctor's family; he had met few people except in his own country neighbourhood, and he suddenly found himself among those who had had a different sort of upbringing. It is no wonder that he was silent and uncomfortable; but fame and popularity are wonderful softeners of that agony of shyness, and if he perhaps kept a little of it deep down inside him, there was no external trace of it. He was perfectly natural with all whom he met, and if he liked them he was soon friendly and hearty with them. He was helped by a wonderful unselfconsciousness. He seemed to take himself for granted, at once a supreme player of his game, and, off the field, as an ordinary person, and did not bother his head about what impression he made. He was far better known by sight than any man in England. Long after his cricketing days were over, he had only to pass through a village street in a motorcar for windows to be thrown up and fingers to be pointed, but he seemed, and really was, as nearly as possible unaware of it, unless perhaps his admirer was a small child, to whom he liked to wave his hand. This unselfsconsciousness pervaded his whole existence. He had come, as has been said, from a home comparatively countrified and uncultivated; he kept, to some extent at least, its manners and its way of speech all his life. He mixed constantly with those who were, in a snobbish sense, his superiors and had other ways and other manners, and I do not believe that he ever gave such things a thought. He recognised different standards in the houses he stayed at, to the extent that there were some to which he ought to take his 'dancing-pumps', and that was all. He liked friendliness and cheerfulness wherever he met it; he was ready to give it himself, and never thought of anything else that could be demanded of him.

A whole bottle of champagne was a mere nothing to him; having consumed it he would go down on all fours, and balance the bottle on the top of his head and rise to his feet again. Nothing could disturb that magnificent constitution, and those who hoped by a long and late sitting to shorten his innings next day often found themselves disappointed. His regular habit while cricketing was to drink one large whisky and soda, with a touch of angostura bitters, at lunch, and another when the day's play had ended; this allowance he never varied or exceeded till the evening came, and, despite his huge frame, though he never dieted, he ate sparingly.

He carried his practical joking into the realms of cricket, as when, according to a well-known story, he caused the batsman to look up at the sky to see some imaginary birds, with the result that the poor innocent was blinded by the sun and promptly bowled. With this we come to one of the most difficult questions about W. G. – did he at all, and, if so, how far, overstep the line which, in a game, divides fair play from sharp practice? There is one preliminary thing to say, namely that there is no absolute standard in these matters, and that standards differ with times and societies. The sportsmen of the early nineteenth century did, naturally and unblushingly, things that would be considered very unsportsmanlike nowadays. In those days everything was a 'match': each party must look after himself; it was play or pay, and the devil take the hindermost. He would never have dreamed of purposely getting in the way of a fieldsman who might otherwise have caught him, but to shout cheerfully to that fieldsman, 'Miss it', was – at any rate in a certain class of cricket – not merely within the law, but rather a good joke.

The law was the law, though in his intense keenness he could not wholly rid himself of the idea that it was sometimes unjustly enforced against him; what the law allowed was allowable. It was always worth appealing; if the umpire thought a man was out l.b.w., it did not matter what the bowler thought. 'You weren't out, you know,' he was sometimes heard to say to a retiring batsman against whom he had appealed, and thought no shame to do so: everything was open and above board; if the umpire decided you were out – and he sometimes decided wrong – that was all about it. He wanted desperately to get the other side out, and any fair way of doing so was justifiable; he never stooped to what he thought was a mean way. No man knew the law better, and it could seldom be said against him that he was wrong, but rather that he was too desperately right.

His early cricket had been played with a father and three elder brothers who were going to stand no nonsense from the younger ones. The boy was taught to behave himself, and this meant, amongst other things, to stick to the rules. It was natural enough that when he grew older he expected other players to behave themselves too. It may be said that he did not sufficiently distinguish between big points and small ones, but the answer is that, where cricket was concerned, there was for W. G. no such thing as a small point. It might seem trivial to more easy-going or more flexibily minded persons; never to him; and if things were not, as he thought, just right, he came out bluntly and impetuously with his opinion.

Crime or Folly (1937)

One day last week I was reading, perhaps with rather a drowsy eye, the account of a match at squash rackets when suddenly an arresting phrase woke me up. I gathered that So-and-so might have won but for making 'shots of almost unbelievable folly at moments of great importance'. I experienced an instant feeling of sympathy for the poor fellow. I also thought that here was a writer who could enrich my limited vocabulary against the next time when I had to describe the missing of a putt. So I read on to find the same player accused of 'egregious error' and 'ill-timed eccentricities'. By now I was almost to tears on his behalf, but still I persisted. I wanted to discover, however painful it might be, what were the dreadful things he had done. Furthermore, since I have a bad habit of translating everything into terms of golf, there might be some analogy between his crimes and those which the more black-hearted of golfers commit.

His chief offences appeared to have been two; the first that he tried to take a ball when he ought to have asked for a let; the second that being in one game within a stroke of victory he served – my pen falters in the transcription – 'straight on to the tin'. Heaven forbid that I should endeavour to excuse one of such palpably criminal instincts. Doubtless he deserved his fate, and yet in other ways he may be a most respectable man and I am still sorry for him.

When I come to turning this sad story into golfing language I am not sure that everything can be explained by 'unbelievable folly'. There seems to be a distinction between the two mistakes, to use a miserably small word. To serve the ball on the tin at game-ball is like topping the ball into a bunker in front of our noses at dormy one when the other fellow is really in trouble. It is the most deplorable stroke and one which the Fates will not forgive, but is it, strictly speaking, an act of folly? Poor wretches that we are, we do not do it on purpose, and not even our foursome partner, justly incensed though he be, can think that. It was simply that we would not act up to our doubtless admirable intentions. On the other hand, the not asking for a let was a deliberate act. A possible golfing equivalent is the playing of a ball out of a puddle when we might lift it out instead. That would be a folly, even if of an heroic nature.

Golf being a cold, calculating sort of game gives perhaps more scope for folly than any other. We have all the time in the world to make up our minds as to what is the wise thing to do and then we do the foolish one. Yet even so it is often hard to say exactly how foolish it was. We see a man go out for a long carry over a bunker or burn when he is playing the one off two, and we say in a furious whisper, 'The man's a fool! Play short, you idiot!' We do not know, however, what is going on inside his head nor how frightened he may be of a short pitch. He may have coolly calculated all the chances and decided that he was more likely to get over with a brassie than with a mashie. I once saw a player at Westward Ho! who was dormy one in the semi-final of the championship; although his enemy had been in all manner of trouble, he lashed out at his second with a brassie and he jumped the burn! That looked an incredibly rash action, and yet he thought before he did it, and who shall say that he did not think rightly? He knew himself and the spectator did not.

Last year in a championship at Deal I saw a respected and illustrious friend of mine apparently take leave of his wits. He too was dormy one; both he and his enemy were at the foot of the bank in two, and a five would in all probability be good enough for the half and the match. Every individual hair on my head stood straight on end when I saw him, instead of knocking the ball up the slope with a putter or a straight-faced iron, take out his mashie niblick. It was a horrid little pitch to play at such a moment, and, sure enough, he fluffed it and lost the hole. When he had ultimately won the match at the 21st I ventured with infinite delicacy to ask what on earth had possessed him. He answered that he had had such bad 'jitters' on the green that he felt as if he would miss the globe if he took his putter. Only those who have suffered from that fearful complaint can fully appreciate his action, which, though unsuccessful, may yet have been the wisest in the circumstances.

Last summer at St Andrews I was very properly rebuked by another eminent friend while watching the final of the Amateur championship. In the first round Ferrier held a good lead from Hector Thomson after the 13th hole. Then he cut his tee shot over the wall out of bounds at the Long-hole-in and so gave his hardly pressed adversary a needed and heartening opportunity. I stigmatised it as a foolish shot at such a moment, but my friend would not have it. A man, he said, playing as well as Ferrier was then, got into a frame of mind of such concentrated confidence that he never thought of the possibility of going out of bounds. To do so might admittedly be disastrous, but even so it was much more than worth the risk to attain so happy a state. Being myself of a timorous and pessimistic frame of mind I could not speak from experience, but there was at any rate a good deal to be said for the contention and I withdrew the 'foolish'.

It is a shameful thing to confess, but I once very nearly called a Major-General foolish. He and I were partners in a war-time match – not a very important one – played by foursomes, and on the first green he was left with a putt of between two-foot and three-foot for the half. Our opponents, as all well-disciplined young soldiers should, exclaimed smartly in chorus, 'That will do, Sir'; but the General insisted on trying that putt, and he missed it by several inches. His was a noble action, worthy of the best traditions of the British Army, but from a base commercial standpoint it was not a wise one, for the enemy could offer to give us no more putts and we missed all the ones that we were not given.

Giving Up the Game (1945)

Whatever the game, many give it up when the decline of their powers is still a slow and gentle movement. I once asked the late Stanley Jackson whether he played much cricket nowadays, and with that perfect candour and the quality of taking himself for granted which made one of his great charms, he replied that he did not; 'the fact is I don't play so well as I used to and I don't like it'. Then he added something like these words: 'I play once a year at Harrow and I generally go in and make fifty or sixty runs and then when I go on to bowl they won't take me off because they know I shall be so stiff that I could never go on again.' I can see the spot where he said it, on a golf course in Cheshire, and it struck me as so simple and engaging that the words there and then burnt themselves into my memory and I can almost guarantee their accuracy.

Nobody can like it, when he finds himself not so good as he was, but some dislike it much more acutely than others. Presumably the ideal is to dislike it so little, or to like the game so much more, that even an eighteen handicap or a series of ducks and missed catches make 'a sundown splendid and serene'; but that is a great deal to ask. A little allowance must be made for the vanity of poor frail human nature, and in golf at any rate I have observed that those who go on the longest have had, as a rule, no very high standard of achievement from which to fall. The octogenarian foursomes, of which we sometimes hear, are seldom composed of old internationals. It is not, I hope, unbearably sentimental to say that there is something sad in watching a once fine player beginning to slip. I remember a conversation with Harold Hilton at Hoylake, on the evening when the side to play for England against Scotland was being chosen. He remarked that in a year or two people would be saying, 'Hilton – h'm – is he good enough?' It sounded in my worshipping ears a kind of blasphemy uttered by a deity against himself. Could such a time ever come? And yet it did, as it now appears, almost in a flash. But that very great golfer continued to play the game when the little jump on to the toes and the follow-through seemed the same as before; only the remorseless, realistic ball refused to go.

That is the braver course and surely the happier, but this 'menace of the years' affects different people in different ways and sometimes in, to me at any rate, unexpected ways. Those whom I imagined going on for ever make a sudden break, and those who, as it seemed, could hardly bear the descent, go philosophically topping and slicing down the hill. I can recall one whom I should have thought as nearly as might be untouched by vain regrets, and yet he gave up early and utterly. He never tired of looking on, with a club under his arm, but only in the far distance, when he believed nobody by, could he be seen now and then to play a shot with it, nor, I think, would it have been tactful to admit that one had played the spy on his privacy. More enviable was another, a great player in his day and one of perennial keenness, who went on playing in a green old age, hardly realising what had befallen him. He still experimented with clubs of vast weight, because some lusty young driver used them; still walked on and on expecting to find his ball, long after he had passed it. He must have been puzzled now and then, but I doubt if he ever clearly drew the painful deduction from the obvious facts.

There was one golfer whom in this regard I admired more than any other, and since I have nothing but praise to give, why should I not name him? This was the late Mr Mure Fergusson. In his prime he had not suffered bad players very gladly, but when he was old and stiff and full of rheumatism, and had to receive many strokes from those to whom he had once given them, he went on his way round the links with a dour cheerfulness. He recounted with grim enjoyment how his small caddie had declared that he might yet become a player if he could learn not to drop his shoulder. He even adopted the mental attitude of the poor and lowly so far as to murmur at the unfairness of certain bunkers into which his best shots found their way. I could not help reflecting how tersely he would once have received such complaints, but I expressed the deepest sympathy and felt it.

But let me count the blessings of giving up. They are not to be despised and are reasonably free from the reproach of sour grapes. At least some of the fun, much of the companionship and all the friendliness remain. Golf drives a harder bargain with the retired than does any other game. He cannot sit at his ease in the pavilion or on a stand, but must pursue the players over a broken and difficult country. He comes to watch more and more on inner lines of communication. He resigns himself to the knowledge that the holes at the far end of the course are not for him; he must be content with ghoulish hopes of an agonising finish about the 16th and 17th greens. If he inclines to be censorious in his comments he cannot be put to the proof; no one can say to him in effect, 'Go and do better yourself'. I do not think, however, that he does grow fiercer but rather milder. His judgement is apt to err on the side of admiring very ordinary strokes, since it is tinged by his knowledge that he can no longer make any strokes at all. It is so hard to maintain a wholly impersonal standard of criticism. He falls unconsciously into a second childhood of making pyrotechnic noises at any normal drive. The fact that he could once make such a drive himself may be obvious to him from well-known landmarks on the course but he does not believe it for all that. It is an excess of humility and not of arrogance that makes him a less and less trustworthy judge of others. He is so humble as to mistake anything that glitters, however faintly, for gold. I would put little faith in him now as a chooser of teams.

For the retired warrior there are no anxieties, no agonies, no thwarted ambitions, no wretched little jealousies, no bitter regrets. Never again will he toss and tumble, thinking of the match that is before him on the morrow. No black demon of a missed putt from the match that is past will crouch beside his pillow to arouse him at midnight. He will not watch his conqueror going on gaily from round to round and murmur to himself that that is where he ought to be. There will be no penitence for having been cross, for as far as the game is concerned he need never be cross any more; no miserable pretence of being a good loser, for there is nothing to lose.

On the morning of the match the course had always a hard, unsympathetic look. The greens so beautifully trim and smooth seemed like places of public execution made ready, on to which the criminal must step out with a show of bravery at the appointed hour. The very flags blowing out straight from their sticks spoke to him of the wind as a personal enemy. Fate still hangs brooding heartless over the course but him she cannot touch. The voice of the starter is no longer the voice of doom. There will be heaps of slain ere the bloody day is out, but he will still be alive in inglorious security.

Put Her in the Woodshed (1941)

Do the young people enjoy children's parties? I am sure I hated them, if not quite so heartily as I expected to when I was being made ready. I can still experience a nightmare in which I am skulking in a corner, hoping to avoid detection, and a large kind hostess comes up and says to me, 'You'll play, I'm sure, won't you?' There was something, though very little, to be said for musical chairs. There was about it a competitive, even an athletic element: a certain interest in sailing as near the wind as possible, in hovering to the very verge of the law over each chair, and dashing tempestuously through the danger zone at the end of the line. But it is all too horrible to think of. In any case by the time my sister was of a children's party age I was too old and it is far pleasanter to recall our domestic games with our cousins who lived almost next door.

There was one for which I still feel a great tenderness, the leaf-catching game, played in the dusk on some windy afternoon just before tea, in the autumn or early winter. It combined the virtues of competition and the team spirit, for we divided into two sides, and victory went to the side which caught most leaves from a big beech tree in given time. The stronger the wind the farther into the deep field we went, and yet there was always a chance for some cunning fielder close in, who would ever and anon snap up a leaf that did no more than totter off its branch. That might be profitable but the real chivalry of the game consisted in the high leaves that came whirling in their tens and twenties before a fierce blast. After that there was perhaps a pause; the wind had gone rumbling away into the distance; there was silence and not a leaf stirred. A single one would come twisting this way and that, first it seemed the prey of one side, then of the other, and then would flutter to the ground ere it was reached or take an upward leap overhead.

Suddenly the wind would come roaring back from far away and once more we were all a-tiptoe. It was a great game but tantalising and trying to the honesty. We called the score aloud at each leaf caught and often there would come a triumphant cry of 'Fifteen' followed by 'No – sorry – only fourteen.' The hand had closed on the leaf; there could be no doubt it was there and yet somehow the hand when opened was empty. That little shrivelled imp of mischief had escaped after all. Victory was ardently, almost savagely fought for, but there was an aesthetic pleasure that was better than sordid gain, a high running catch over the head, or a low one, taken at the last dying flutter, made us 'higher than the angels'. Tea grew cold, jam waited, grown-up voices, hortatory or persuasive, summoned us in, but the match had to be fought out to the last brave leaf.

I make no claim to have been a champion, though I suppose that from greater height and length of reach I ought to have sucked some advantage. There were other games in which that advantage was obvious so that I must be handicapped accordingly. Such was the ancient Belgian game of *chole*, which I introduced after reading about it in Andrew Lang's historical chapter in the Badminton golf book. It is an admirable game, at least for persons who cannot hit very far, and my handicap consisted in a left-handed iron. The principle of the game is simple. It begins like bridge with a bidding match, each side undertaking to reach a certain goal, such as a tree, in so many innings, and the side making the lowest bid having the first attempt. An innings consists of so many strokes forward, in our case two, and after it the other side is allowed one stroke, which goes by the name of the *decholade*. It can be played in any direction that the *decholeur* pleases, his object being to put the ball into the most odious situation within reach. Thus the game possesses a quality in which golf, with all its virtues, is lacking, namely the directly hostile attack by one side on the other. To steer the enemy ball into some spot whence it is, humanly speaking, inextricable, is to taste one of the most fiendish joys that life has to offer. Sometimes this was geographically easy, but at others, when the ground lay comparatively open, the *decholade* demanded both cunning and skill. There was a stroke favoured by one school, which consisted in hitting the ball a downward blow on the head with the back of the iron and thus driving it underground. If the ground was soft enough it was very effective but it was a perilous stroke, for unless it was delivered with great exactitude the ball bobbed up into the air, the *decholade* was wasted and the match as good as lost. The ideal of all *decholeurs* was to put the ball into the woodshed. That represented the 'winning gallery' and if ever the ball was in it hope was abandoned. Even as spectators at a football match are sometimes worked up to exclaim, 'Kill him' or 'Stamp on his head', so our most bloodthirsty cry, giving vent to every instinct of savagery, was 'Put her in the woodshed!'

A Musical Cure (1935)

'If music be the food of golf, play on.' So spoke Orsino in the play, or if it was not exactly that it was something very like it. Doubtless he was alluding to the necessity for rhythm, that indefinable and elusive something the presence of which we recognise in the swings of the great, while we are too painfully aware of its absence in our own. It comes and goes and, as we get older and stiffer, it is apt to go for ever, but if by chance we have a fair day we are conscious that it has come faintly fluttering back, and for a moment we can 'almost hear the beating of its wings'. There is a traditional prescription for its recapture, which consists in swinging the club to a waltz tune. I had tried it long since, as I must have tried almost everything once, but had forgotten all about it till I came across it again in the work of a highly distinguished American teacher, Mr Seymour Dunn. So away I went to a secret valley, a very muddy one in the season of rain, where no human eye could see my contortions nor human ear hearken to my carolings, and 'Gad, there I was,' as Jos Sedley once observed, 'singing away like – a robin.'

There are presumably many waltz tunes, but I could only think of two. The first was that eminently languorous one, title to me unknown, from *The Merry Widow*; the second, if it may be named with respect, was the tune of the hymn called 'Happy birds that sing and fly', which at least sufficiently resembles a waltz. Between these two I was forced to alternate. I am no musician any more than I am a dancer, and prefer, if I sing at all, to have my notes drowned by the running waters of my morning bath or still better by the rattle and roar of a railway train, supposing that I have a carriage to myself. I fancy my singing, though here I may be flattering myself, to be not unlike that of Bertie Wooster when he daily gave vent to 'Sonny Boy'. For golfing purposes, however, that is rather an advantage than otherwise. Singers of this type, that is to say having naturally bad taste, no voice and an imperfect ear, are given to a slow and sentimental sweetness long drawn out, and this lends itself admirably to the drowsy swing which we ought to cultivate.

I remember in the early stages of the war being at Aldershot when Sir Walford Davies (he was only Dr then) kindly came down to teach the new army how to sing and form regimental choirs. He told his pupils not to sing 'in the sloppy, Bank Holiday style', and a general and sheepish grin showed that the shot had gone home. Then he made them sing the Old Hundredth, which they did so lugubriously as to evoke the protest, 'Now you know you wouldn't sing "How's your lady friend" like that.' Next 'The Old Folks at Home' was greeted with the friendly sarcasm, 'Oh, come, sloppier than that!' Finally they were drilled into singing with a briskness and crispness that a little while before would have seemed incredible.

Sir Walford was clearly in the right, if it be not impertinent to say so; but I feel like Bob Acres when he refused to follow Sir Lucius's duelling precepts, and said firmly, 'By my valour, I will stand edgeways'. Music is one thing and golf is another, and for the purposes of this golfing cure I doubt if it be possible to sing too sloppily. Let the patient get all the intolerable pathos he can out of 'One little hut among de bushes,' 'When will I hear de bees a-humming', and all the other words of that heart-breaking and beloved song. He can scarcely have too many tears in his voice, hardly be too maudlin, so long as nobody can hear him. If he tries to be too brisk he may soon be snatching and snapping at the ball as badly as ever.

A waltz tune is, no doubt, the best, but I am disposed, though diffidently, to think that almost any tune will do good, so long as we sing or whistle it with sufficient languor. It is not necessary to go on with *The Merry Widow* till it drives us mad. One important thing is not to take a deep breath at the top of the swing and come down on the ball with too violent a burst of melody. Another is not to stop as we reach the ball but to finish, of course in a chaste and classical attitude, with the music still flowing evenly from our lips. I ought to add that Mr Dunn prescribes the waltz tune primarily for acquiring a rhythmic swing with no ball there. When there is a ball and we are inclined to press and jerk at it, he suggests a different musical remedy – namely, to 'whistle a continuous, low, even note all the way through the swing'. He may be right; he probably is, but this whistling of one note is by comparison a dreary and for some of us a difficult business. Do let us have our tune and get a little fun out of the treatment!

It may be observed that with singular modesty I have said nothing of the effect of this cure upon the particular patient in question. Well, hope does not spring as it did, and to hit the ball nowadays, if he ever does hit it, appears rather an ironical circumstance. Yet I will say this, that now and again he did seem to acquire some vestige of a pause at the top of the swing and actually did follow through. Moreover, and this is always a cheerful sign, the remedy was reasonably effective on the second day, whereas most remedies only last for one. The weather and the valley being now alike unspeakable he is wondering whether a musical treatment indoors would be good for putting. There might be a measure of compensation in putting at the drawing-room table-legs when the household insists on listening to Bach on the wireless. But these musical people are so fussy; they say 'Hush', and besides I doubt if Bach is quite the man for the job.

Dickens in Time of War (1915)

The anniversary of Charles Dickens, who was born on the seventh of February a hundred and three years ago, is one that should never be forgotten, even though there is no peculiar appropriateness in remembering it at such times as the present. We can imagine, indeed, how, had such a crisis arisen in his day, Dickens would have flung himself into the task of raising men and money: how he would have been here, there, and everywhere, reading, acting, speaking, and making spare time in which to shoulder a musket himself and drill with a fiery enthusiasm; how he would have denounced the crimes of the Germans in Belgium, and what a trumpet-call to the whole world his voice would have been. But, although he wrote at a time when Waterloo was a living memory, and his young days at Chatham might have given him a love of the army, there is in fact very little of war to be found in his books. There is fine fighting in Dickens, but it is the street fighting of revolution, the burning of Newgate in the Gordon Riots, or the bloody sea rising in St Antoine, when, at the beating of the drum, with Madame Defarge at their head, the mob fall on Foulon and drag him to the lamp. As regards real soldiers Joe Willett enlisted and came back with an empty sleeve from 'the defence of the Salwanners', and in the story of Dick Doubledick from *The Seven Poor Travellers* there is fighting in India, at Badajoz, and at Waterloo. But that story, according to modern taste, is very far from representing Dickens at his best; it verges both on the sentimental and the melodramatic, and if we want soldiers we would far rather turn to the review in *Pickwick*.

So on this particular seventh of February our reflections are really much the same as they might be in a year of peace. We try to estimate the position that Dickens occupies with the readers of today, and wonder, not without some misgivings, whether there are quite so many people as there used to be, and ought to be, capable of naming correctly The Brick Lane Branch of the United Grand Junction Ebenezer Temperance Association. There are at least some very cheering pieces of evidence that may be adduced. In the first place Mr Henry Dickens has given splendid proof of the power of his father's name by the large sum which he has collected for the Red Cross Society's fund by giving readings from his works. The statistics of circulating libraries show that *David Copperfield* is one of the most sought after of all books; a play founded upon it is now running a successful career at His Majesty's Theatre, and *Barnaby Rudge* has lately been adapted to the film. Yet another artist has produced a book of drawings of Dickens's London, and yet another dauntless commentator has solved to his own satisfaction the mystery of Edwin Drood.

Perhaps, however, the best evidence of how potent is still the spell of Dickens, and how widely diffused the affection for him, is to be found in the pages of the magazine called *The Dickensian*, which is the organ of the Dickens Fellowship. The February number reproduces from *The Times* that delightful little account, in a letter written from the front by a captain of the Royal Artillery, of how he gave a recital of *A Christmas Carol*. The recital was announced in camp orders, and 300 men had to be turned away from the doors because there was no more room. 'All through the dialogue,' says the writer, 'the men (I could feel it) simply sat breathless, hoping against hope that Scrooge would turn up trumps. And then, at the last words "And therefore I'm going to raise your salary" there was an extraordinary outburst of relief – laughter and spontaneous applause.'

In the same number of *The Times* are reports of Fellowship meetings, not only from various places in the United Kingdom,

but from Toronto, Winnipeg, Sydney, Hobart, Philadelphia, and
Bethlehem, Pa. At the last named place *A Christmas Carol* was
acted as a short four-act play by the boys of the Moravian Parochial School – a title which suggests Mr Bumble – and an original
composition called 'Christmas in Dickens's Land – a Reverie', was
read aloud. It is easy to smile at these ebullitions of fervour, and
some of us may very well have a great love for Dickens, and very
small desire for such reunions. Hero worship, which is essentially
the same as our own but is just a little less critical or more demon-
strative, is apt to strike us as rather tiresome and ridiculous. But it
is after all but a poor enthusiasm that shies at a little difference of
taste, and people may be men and brothers even though they like
little Nell better than Dick Swiveller and little Dombey better
than Toots. 'Hooroar for the principle', as Mr Samuel Weller
once remarked, and the principle is that of reading and loving
Dickens.

It lies with all who have embraced it to see that this principle is
maintained in time to come, and there is one way of doing so that
is too frequently neglected – namely, the reading of Dickens
aloud to children when they are quite young. Parents and guard-
ians, in considering the question of reading aloud, are apt to be too
frightened at the prospect of a few obviously grown-up passages
and to underrate the possibilities of judicious skipping. Yet, if they
have been lucky in their own upbringing they should remember
the joy of a scene picked out here and there – Mr Winkle and his
horse, or the drive in Mr Barkis's cart, or the cricket match between Dingley Dell and All Muggleton. They should bear in mind,
moreover, that because children do not enjoy quite in the same
way as their elders, it by no means follows that they do not enjoy
just as much. Mr Boffin probably did not appreciate in all its
aspects the genius of Gibbon, but he thought that Vittle-us and
Commodious were stunning. If every lover of Dickens were to
read to his children on this seventh of February the adventures of
Mr Pickwick at the Chatham review, he would be laying by for
them a nest-egg of happiness; and he would also be doing something of his duty in handing on the torch.

A Triumphal Progress
(1929)

Walter Hagen won the Open championship here [Muirfield] today for the second year in succession and the fourth time all told. He won it by six strokes from the second man in a total score of 292, made up of three 75s and a 67, a magnificent score on so long a course with such difficult greens and, as regards the last rounds, in such trying weather. He was not only the greatest golfer in the field but in a golfing sense the greatest man in the field. If the epithet great can ever be properly applied to a game player, then it is Walter Hagen's due. Throughout the last two days of this championship he towered over all the other players of his own country (Bobby Jones was not among them). He seems as regards score play to have slipped back a little, but put him on a British seaside course with a seaside wind, and he has something that none of his brother professionals quite possess. He can hit the ball lower through the wind; he can stand stiller on the green than any of them; when it comes to getting out of trouble he is without a peer. He has never before in this country played as well as he has this time.

From the very start Hagen played like a conqueror in the third round. He dealt with the storm like an artist and his touch on the windswept greens was beautiful. His start, 4, 4, 3, 3, 4, 4 was perfect for six holes and he had added to his lead on both Englishmen (Alliss and Mitchell). At the short 7th he lay very badly in a bunker and had to hit with might and main instead of gently

94

stroking the ball out as is his wont. He shooed it out and nearly holed for his three. Two steady-going fives gave him a 37 and he went on 4, 4, 5. So far he had been almost dull. Now came the old Hagen touch. He tried his low shot to the 13th, cut it a little too fine and was bunkered. He chipped it out with complete unconcern to about six yards and holed the putt. What a contrast to poor Mitchell's hole twenty minutes earlier! One took four putts, the other one putt.

Hagen had a thoroughly futile and uncharacteristic six at the 14th without touching a bunker, but promptly set himself right with a grand three at the 15th where his iron shot into the teeth of the wind made one catch one's breath. 4, 4, 5 with a bunker at the last hole finished a great round and put Hagen in a very strong position, four strokes ahead of Alliss and five ahead of Mitchell.

Now for his triumphal progress in the final round, for that is what it was, as everyone who was watching it very well knew. He holed a good putt for a three at the 2nd and went careering joyously along until he was two under fours for seven holes. At the 8th he deliberately drove far to the right into the rough, having indicated his intention by having the crowd moved. This bold stroke gave him a short-cut to the hole; he got a good lie, played a perfect picture of an approach within two yards, and holed the putt. He was three under fours, and had obtained his winning lead by wonderfully brilliant golf.

Now came the second phase, that of hanging on. He ceased to be brilliant and made a certain number of mistakes but always cut his losses with admirable coolness and judgement. At the 9th he hooked his second and his ball lay tight under the wall.

He produced a left-handed club, much as a conjurer produces a goldfish out of a hat, and played a high pitch to the edge of the green. He took three putts and a six, but that was 35, and he led the two Englishmen by ten strokes apiece. 4, 5, 5, for the next three was nothing out of the common, and at the 13th he made the very same mistake he had made in the morning. If it had been anybody else, one might have felt a cold thrill of apprehension, but not with Hagen. Once again he pitched up beautifully and got a four that was nearly a three, and then, as if to show what he could really do when he tried, got the grandest of fours at the 14th, which against the wind could not be reached in under three shots.

He was bunkered at the 15th and bunkered again at the 18th. The only question was whether he would lose one shot or no shot. That he should lose two was not credible. 5, 4, 5, 5 with a short putt missed at the last hole made him 40 home. By four o'clock the championship was over. What anybody else might do was merely a matter of places in the prize list . . .

Nailed Shoes over Waterloo Bridge (1925)

It is to be hoped that at this time of year a number of people read once more the account of the Christmas journey to Dingley Dell. At any rate, I do; I find it does something to fortify me against the festive rigours of the season. When I was thus reading it yet again, it occurred to me to describe a winter journey that hardy golfers used to make, not once but many times. It may not appear much of a one; yet it came back to me with a sentimental thrill, and since it was before the days of motor-cars, and even of tubes, it seems fully as distant as any coach drive. It was the journey that we used to make to Woking on wintry Sunday mornings towards the end of last century.

How easy it is to get there now, or to its pleasant neighbours Worplesdon and West Hill, in somebody else's motor-car! It was then an event in itself, made up of several adventures. First of all there was the getting to Waterloo at an inclement hour. In his book *Fly-fishing* Lord Grey of Fallodon gives a quite delightful account of going early to Waterloo, bound for the Itchen or the Test. He saw with the eyes of true romance that the hansoms then to be found 'seemed quite different from the hansoms abroad at more lively hours'. I did not take a hansom, but, since I lived in the Temple, I walked over Waterloo Bridge, and I do not think it is a purely romantic memory that the pavement on that bridge was of a character different from that of all other pavements. It was of granite, which to one who walked in nailed shoes was of an icy slipperiness. If Mr Wordsworth had worn nailed shoes and walked over Waterloo instead of Westminster Bridge, he never could have written his sonnet, for he would have been wholly occupied in not tumbling on his distinguished nose. To be late and to have to run for the train, clubs in hand, was a very definite adventure.

Trains were still trains, even in this era of romance, but there is something of old enchantment in the memory that we got cheap blue tickets for half-a-crown and no more, and travelled in dear, varnished second-class carriages with red cushions.

The journey itself was sociable and friendly enough, but when we had passed Byfleet and set down our cargo of golfers bound for the pinewoods of New Zealand, we began to fret in our seats, to get our clubs down from the rack, and to look on our neighbour as our natural enemy. Once we got into Woking Station it was a case of *sauve qui peut*; there was a wild rush for the brake and devil take the hindermost. I can see in my mind's eye one particular pair of coat-tails flying down the platform. The owner always wore them, I think, as a badge of divided allegiance; he hunted with the Whaddon Chase on the Saturday and played golf on the Sunday. How pleasant it would be to see them again flying away from the first tee! They always got there first and certainly never kept anyone back; it was their partner who had the hard time of it. I remember to have taken an eminent golfer for his first visit to the course, of which he has since become a permanent feature. He looked with a certain placid surprise at the flight down the platform, and remarked, 'It is beneath the dignity of a Scottish gentleman to run'. So we walked, and had the last and slowest cab all to ourselves.

Even if we condescended to run and thus got a place in the brake the journey was by no means over, for we could not drive up to the club-house, or indeed anywhere near it. We were turned out by the roadside and scrambled up a slope across a tract of heather, then across a railway bridge, then through a little wood of hollies, and then we were there. It was possible by great activity to gain some places in this flight across the heather. There was a pleasant sensation of catching and passing exhausted adversaries in the last lap of some imaginary three-mile race. The coat-tails alone were invincible. They were always in the van.

Moreover, all these processes had to be repeated on the way home. It was a wrench to turn out of a nice warm club-house and paddle across the heather in the dark to where the brake lamps awaited us. The main path was flanked, if I remember rightly, by ditches, and there was even a legend of one who fell in and had to be rescued. That was after a match played there by the team of 'Scottish Gentlemen' who used to invade us, but I daresay it is not true, or only true in a Pickwickian sense. At any rate, by the time one had squeezed into the brake and rumbled to the station, and stopped at Byfleet, Weybridge, Walton, Esher, Surbiton, Wimbledon, Clapham Junction, and Vauxhall, and tumbled back over the granite bridge, one felt one had done a good day's work.

It *was* a good day's work, but there were many people anxious to do it. The star of fir trees and heather had not then arisen to lighten the darkness of London golfers. Men judged things by Tooting standards, and we and our neighbours of New Zealand were unique. It was rumoured that the waiting list at Woking was so long that when at last the Committee proposed to elect a candidate he was generally found to be dead. So to be a member was to be fortunate, and the course was just as pleasant as it is now. Some of the greens have been moved farther on: the holly trees have been cut back from the second hole: the long, bare stretches of 'Harley Street' have been broken up with bunkers, whereby the hole has become far easier, but the old charm is still about it. It is still worth tumbling into a ditch to play there, and I have written this dull little account of it to please myself and in the faint hope that my friend of the flying tails may read it and like to remember.

More Strokes, More Fun (1932)

The tearing up of a card is generally regarded as a rather discreditable business, showing at once vanity and pusillanimity in the tearer; and I must say that I do feel something more of a man when I have gone on to the bitter end and handed in the horrid thing. Circumstances, however, alter cases; there are occasions when, if only for the sake of the players behind, we are almost justified in the cowardly act, and I am about to write of one.

As a rule, when a golfer tears up a card he does so not merely figuratively, but literally, and no one but his marker knows the exact facts. A card has now come into my hands which, I think, its owner must have intended to destroy. He did not, however, and his marker first secreted it and then passed it on to another who, thinking that it might be useful, gave it to me. The whole business is, as you will perceive, a shady, if not a positively dishonourable, one. I feel rather ashamed of it; but so poignant a 'human document' as this card cannot be allowed to lie hidden. So, with all due precautions of anonymity as to player and course, it shall be set out.

The score was compiled in a qualifying competition on a well-known seaside course, and here it is as far as it goes:

Out: 10, 12, 9, 9, 10, 7, 11, 9, 8
Home: 12, 17, 12, 9, 20, 8.

That is to say, the player took 85 to go out and he had taken 78 for six holes on the way home when he gave up the unequal struggle. Statisticians will note that he took double figures at eight out of the fifteen holes played, and that his average score for a hole was $10\frac{13}{15}$. There appears to be some doubt whether the tally was duly kept. Both marker and player, though persons of the highest probity, may have grown a little tired, and one who played behind them declares that in the twenty recorded for the fourteenth hole 'air shots were not counted'. I entirely dissociate myself from any such slanderous statement, but there it is.

With nothing but the card and the length of the holes to help us, we must employ the methods of Sherlock Holmes if we are to discover anything about the round, and those methods, as Watson found, are easier to admire than to apply. We are probably justified in guessing that the wind rather favoured the player on the way out, but, on the other hand, his later falling off may only have been due to a natural and cumulative fatigue. In those first nine holes, I think, he must have played more or less his normal game, for there are no purple patches, and the two holes at which he took fewest strokes, the 6th and 9th, are both one-shot holes. He holed them in seven and eight respectively and, judged by that standard, his eleven at the 7th, which is 478 yards long, was a noteworthy achievement. On the way home, seventeen was superficially bad at the 11th – a mere 352 yards long – but my recollection is that at this hole there is a deep and cavernous ditch running along the left of the fairway, and once the player is in it, anything might happen. Of course, the twenty at the 14th was a real tragedy, because this is only a one-shot hole of 162 yards. Heaven forbid that I should call it an easy three; it is not that, and especially not in a wind, but it is a little hard to understand where there is enough trouble to account for an 'approximated' twenty.

No praise can be too high for the way in which, after this calamity, the player pulled himself together and did his second eight of the round, and that not this time at a one-shotter. This makes it all the sadder that he never holed out the 16th. It is a long and severe hole (510 yards) in hilly country, and I am told that the getting there was a long business. He had almost reached the green when suddenly his courage forsook him. His marker urged him to go on, but he answered quietly that he had 'no chance now', and picked up his ball. So his card only remains a noble fragment. Had he been able to hole the last three holes in thirty-six shots – an average of twelve – he would just have beaten 200. There was a one-shotter coming at the 17th, where another eight might have been hoped for. Could he have done it? That we shall never know. An inscrutable riddle, he mocks us to the end of time.

It chanced that this card was handed to me at the hour of the cocktail in a place where people congregate before luncheon. Several sniggered over it with me, but there was one who took a rather different and more serious view. He said, possibly with some exaggeration, that his golf was of the same quality as that of the man who made the score, and that he and his like got much more pleasure out of the game than did superior persons. Would I, he asked, write an article to that effect, and then, in an inspired moment, he exclaimed: 'More strokes, more fun, there's your title ready-made for you!' So, having adopted his suggestion, I must do the best I can with his subject, but I am not convinced that he is right. His title might be true of cricket, where, roughly speaking, the more strokes the more runs, or, at any rate, the more prolonged the innings. It might be moderately true of lawn tennis. Give me an opponent of exactly my own futile calibre, and we can now and again have quite a long rally by means of our mild little lobs backwards and forwards over the net, which we find exhilarating and enjoyable. Our strokes are contemptible, but they do, during that rally, attain two primary objects of getting the ball over the net and into the court. Our ambitions are strictly limited and are satisfied. On the other hand, the man who takes twelve to a hole at golf is nearly all the time failing miserably to attain his object: a large proportion of those twelve shots must be tops or fluffs, unless, indeed, they are, most of them, accounted for by a rapid rain of blows in a bunker which leave the ball *in statu quo*. And surely nobody, except a man who is blind with fury and wants to hit something can enjoy mere unsuccessful thumping.

Admittedly, my friend, taking him at his own valuation, is much more easily pleased than the superior person. One good, honest drive, if he hits one, will give him a greater thrill than a champion will get from a whole round of perfectly struck tee shots. Just to see the ball rise into the air is, for him, something, and when it flies over a tall bunker and disappears into the happy valley beyond he is doubtless ecstatic. Moreover, he is not unduly bothered about hooks and slices; as long as the ball soars, its direction is a secondary consideration. Granted all these things, I still think that his joys are few. 'I 'ate heights,' said a famous professional, who did very few of them. The lowliest must come to hate them when they are part of the regular routine. If an eight could represent perfect play, judged even by the humblest standards, it would be a different matter, but on no course of my acquaintance is there a hole which can be described as 'a good eight hole'.

This is not to say that the very best of golfers must enjoy the game more than the next best, and so on down the scale. I do not believe that for a moment, but I do say that beyond a certain pitch of badness golf cannot be very much fun. Probably the exceedingly steady and trustworthy golfer with a handicap of five or six gets as much pleasure as most people. Within his powers he makes a great many good shots, he gets a little the best of it in match-making, he wins, by means of his steadiness, a large proportion of matches and half-crowns. He is not tortured by mad ambitions to be a champion: but stay! is he not? We do not know what is going on inside that old grey head of his, and it may be that he would give all his steadiness just to hit one drive like that young slasher in front. 'See how strangely we men are made!' said Prince Florizel.

Elisha the Founder (1945)

In the portrait before me as I write Elisha Robinson is a strikingly handsome man with a fine dome-like forehead, a straight nose, beetling eyebrows, a firmly set mouth and a full beard. This beard is not positively patriarchal in dimensions since it allows a glimpse of a light-coloured necktie tied in a bow, having about it a tentatively clerical suggestion, well in accord with his coat of broadcloth. He looks, it must be admitted, decidedly formidable, and he had no doubt the capacity for well-timed severity which is necessary for any man who controls a number of men and a large business. At the same time it is not an unkindly face, and it is pleasant to know that his grandchildren were not at all frightened of him and liked to be in his company. One of his granddaughters has the happiest recollections, as of a great treat, of snuggling by his side as he drove his horses to Brighton.

It is clear from some of the little stories of him which survive that he had two invaluable gifts – a sense of humour and a fine unselfconsciousness. One of these stories tells how he was interviewing a possible traveller for the firm and there was an imperfect understanding; the two did not seem to be getting on. 'Look here, Richards,' said Mr Robinson with a sudden inspiration, 'let us change hats.' The traveller had a very small head and the prospective employer a very large one. The exchange was made; each assumed an incongruous headgear and the talk went like a house afire. The other story relates to those visits to Brighton which he made regularly in later life. He always read family prayers, and was one morning in full tide of discourse when his eye was caught by a fine trotting horse as it passed by. He stopped abruptly, walked to the window, watched the trotter along the front and back again, while the family waited in silence, and then went on where he had left off without betraying by the slightest sign that such conduct might be regarded as unusual.

The interest in cricket, so marked in later generations of Robinsons, seems in his case to have been theoretical rather than practical. He clearly approved of it, for in order that one of his grandchildren should begin betimes he had a little bat made in ivory for him to cut his teeth on. His love of horses was deep and ineradicable. He rode daily to his office, and on his visits to Brighton would sometimes send his carriage horses forward and himself make the whole journey from Bristol on horseback. He did not disapprove wholly of racing, as is shown by another agreeable family tradition. One day in London he met two of his sons, who appeared a little disconcerted at the meeting. He asked them where they were going, and they shamefacedly admitted it was to Sandown Park. 'Very well,' said he, 'I'll come with you.'

Of his firm's many activities, Elisha Robinson was, and remained during his life, the chief moving spirit, but it is worth noting as evidence of good organisation that from a comparatively early time in the firm's history he did not find it necessary to be constantly on the spot. His municipal and political activities took up much of his time, but he was a good judge of men and had what some able men never acquire – the power of delegation, so that he could afford to be away knowing that trustworthy people would carry on the work. Moreover he was always, so to speak, in the offing; he was perhaps coming, he might pounce, and one awful legend relates how the office boy, thinking that his master was not coming in for his lunch, devoured the fruit from the garden which made up most of his frugal meal; but alas! his master was only late, and that story may be taken as a parable. Wherever he might be the weight of his hand could be felt from afar, and he was always consulted, as once when he was at a watering place and news was sent him of a fire at the warehouse. His telegraphic answer was brief and to the point. 'Put it out. Robinson.'

As long as he lived he was decidedly and decisively in control, and he laid down one guiding principle which has been remembered and acted on ever since. 'People,' he said, 'remember the quality long after they have forgotten the price.'

Know Your Weakness (1921)

There is one bit of advice the value of which no one would, I imagine, dispute – 'Know thyself'. A golfer may greatly strengthen his match-playing powers by trying and practising, but he can only do so by making the best of himself as he is, not by attempting to turn himself into quite another sort of creature. Not long ago I was watching a very good amateur playing an important match. He looked extraordinarily calm and impassive: he walked after his ball and played his stroke almost as one sleep-walking. With me was one who knew this golfer very well indeed. 'So-and-so thinks so much,' said he, 'about making the crowd think that he does not care, that he sometimes forgets to hit the ball.' That was a very astute observation, and it points out a danger in too consciously schooling ourselves. Very few of us can hope to look as supremely bored as Inman does [at billiards] when his opponent is in the middle of a big break. It springs from natural and inimitable genius. To drill ourselves in external points of behaviour is good in so far as it helps to control the burning fires within us. No man, to take an extreme instance, can foam at the mouth and hurl his club after the ball and yet hope to be in a proper frame of mind for playing his next shot. But it is what is going on inside us that demands our main attention. Beyond a certain point it is only labour lost to put a mask upon our faces. It deceives nobody and distracts us from the main issue.

Knowing our own particular weaknesses, we must treat them

with a combination of tenderness and sternness difficult to attain in exactly the right degree. On some points it is wisest to give way to ourselves. If, for example, we are trying to get into our best form for a particular occasion, the question arises of what sort of practice matches to play. Some people will thrive on a course of fierce fights against players as good or better than themselves. Easygoing games would only make them lazy; the hard struggles tune them up without overstraining them. Certainly there could be no better preparation as long as they are quite sure they can stand it. On the other hand, some players, apart from not being physically strong enough, know that they cannot help taking their practice games too seriously, thinking too much about the winning or losing. They know that should they lose two or three times, even though they have played decently well, it will affect their confidence. If so, they had better perhaps pander to this weakness, and administer to themselves the soothing syrup of a game or two with some nice feeble flattering old gentleman whom they are sure they can beat.

There is just one cheering fact with which the nervous golfer may legitimately comfort himself. It is not the torpid creature with the 'dead nerve', as I have heard it called, who does best in a big match, but rather the highly-strung man who can master himself. It used to be said of one of the greatest advocates at the Bar when in the height of his fame, that the papers would crackle in his hand before a big case, as if he had been a timid junior with his first brief in a county court. The moment he was on his feet nothing more serene and masterly could be imagined. So it is, though in varying degrees, with eminent golfers. Braid has said that he likes to feel a little shaky before a big match, but his kind of shakiness is probably of a comparatively stable kind. Taylor is clearly wrought up, and is so terrible because of the iron grip that he keeps on himself. Those who knew Mr Walter Travis well declared he was a nervous man. Yet when he conquered at Sandwich – and no one ever better deserved to win – there was something diabolic in his apparent calmness. He was Colonel Bogey incarnate.

I suppose the worst temperament for golf, as for any other game, is that which is called the artistic or poetic or imaginative: the worst, that is to say, unless it is most rigorously schooled. The imaginative player has a much greater difficulty than his more stolid brother in keeping strictly to the matter in hand. It is hard for him to make his mind as nearly as possible a perfect blank when he goes up to hit the ball. Well has it been said that 'Golf lends itself readily to the dreaming of scenes in which the dreamer is the hero.' No castles tower higher and more glittering in the air than golfing castles. Before a match or a medal round we play in imagination every single hole. We try to be modest and reasonable: we know that in fact we shall make a mistake or two; and in our dream-cards we mean to introduce a few fives, even perhaps a six for the long hole against the wind, to break our beautiful line of fours and threes. But as we come to each hole we cannot quite bear it: the imaginary mistake gets put off and off, till at the end we have played better than Vardon ever did and gone round in 69 or so. This amusement is so childlike, so far removed from grim reality, that perhaps it does us no great harm. Once we settle down to a real, as opposed to a dream game, we think no more about it. The fatal thing is to play a dream round at the same time as we are playing a real one.

Suppose we are two or three up, we begin to look forward to the winning of the match, say, on the 14th green. We picture our opponent chivalrously congratulating us and saying that we have been altogether too good for him: our friends clapping us cordially on the back with a 'Well played, old chap': spectators looking at us with reverential interest. And just as our dream has reached this perfect consummation, bang goes our adversary's ball against the back of the tin! He has holed a horrible 'gobbling' putt from thirty yards away. Our comparatively short putt which was to have been for the hole is now only for the half, and we shall miss it. We come down to earth with a bump. Our dreams instead of being rosy and golden become black as night. We fancy those friends of ours saying, 'Poor old chap! He was four up at one time and then actually let himself be beaten. He's got no guts

– he can't last.' And at once we set to work to justify those imaginary comments.

For this disease there can be no certain cure. We can only take and shake ourselves – metaphorically – and say, 'Don't be a self-conscious idiot.' And we can try our very hardest to concentrate our minds on each shot as it arises and to take our time. The man who, having had a winning lead, is in process of losing it, is easily recognisable. He walks with a rapid, flurried step: he puffs at his pipe as if his life depended on keeping it alight: he plays the shot as if his one object were to get it over. It *is* a horrid moment, but it will not be made better by hurrying. Now, if ever, is the time to walk slowly and study the putts from both ends and at the same time to play a reasonably bold game. When once a little of our lead has slipped we begin all too soon to think of a halved hole as our highest possible ambition. Of course if we halve enough holes we shall win the match, but to hope for nothing better than halves is not the way to set about getting them.

Here is the sort of thing we have nearly all done and suffered, and seen, too, in the case of other people if we ever watch matches. A, having been four or five up on B, is now only two up with four to go. At the 15th B plays the odd and does not get on to the green: he is in the rough, or even in a bunker. 'Thank God,' thinks A to himself (you can see him thinking it). 'He won't do better than five – I must be able to halve this one, I must be careful.' And he plays a very gingerly shot which just reaches the edge of the green. B promptly puts his niblick shot dead, A takes three putts. He loses the hole, and it is tolerably certain he will lose the match. Could he have controlled himself and his thoughts, he would have played a bolder second and made sure of his four. Then in all probability B would not have put that niblick shot dead or anything like it, for though we are sometimes over-whelmed by the irresistible brilliance of our enemy, it is a rare case. As a rule he plays just as well as we let him and no better.

We must never entirely disregard the art of 'playing to the score', but I am sure we can think too much about it. When our adversary has played the two more it is futile to attempt a long and dangerous carry, but consciously and deliberately to 'play safe' every time we have just a little the best of matters and think the enemy is in difficulties is not the way to win a match. For, first, he may recover, and, secondly, we are not always safe when we mean to be. The shot that is played with no object but to keep the ball in play is just the one we are apt to bungle most sadly. A distinguished golfer of an elder generation said to me the other day that modern players had lost the art of playing the spared shot that was to keep the ball out of trouble and do no more. Perhaps they have: at any rate most of them find it difficult. That particular golfer was once playing in a hurricane of wind at Hoylake. He kept the ball skimming close to the ground and out of harm's way with a straight-faced cleek having a short stiff shaft, while his adversary, attempting more orthodox strokes, was being blown all over the place. 'Mr H.,' said his caddie, 'is not playing a proud game' – and the words have become almost proverbial. To be able to play that sort of golf is a valuable gift, but it is one to be acquired by practice. To attempt it suddenly in a match, when it is unfamiliar, is very dangerous. If it is unsuccessful it will demoralise the player and set the flame of hope burning very brightly in his enemy's breast.

This hypothetical golfer with the poetical and imaginative temperament very often finds prosperity harder to endure than adversity. He is not necessarily deficient in courage, and may fight very well when he is down. But when he gets a winning lead, or at any rate has pulled round a match from a most unpromising situation and given himself a real fighting chance, then is the time that we see him collapse. How many matches have been lost just because the player was impatient to be done with the strain of it and would not give the match time to finish itself!

Against all these and many other temperamental vagaries, the sovereign remedy that is always recommended to us is 'control' – and it is the right one. We cannot hope that the gift of it will suddenly descend on us from above. We must practise it as we would putting, and control does not merely mean refraining from throwing our clubs about, abusing our caddie, and indulging in the 'tut, tut of the eminent divine or the more sulphurous exclamations of the vulgar tongue.' It means, for example, the avoiding of slack, half-hearted shots, and the taking always of a certain amount of trouble, the not running of absurd risks or trying fantastic shots 'just for the fun of it'. In this respect the leading professionals set a wonderful example. If you see Braid playing a foursome with three thoroughly bad players on a course on which he knows every blade of grass, you will notice that he plays every shot with the same serene carefulness that marks him in a championship, studying the line of his putt from the hole if he has any doubt about it. The professional knows that one careless shot begets another, and he cannot afford to get careless. We have not his compelling incentive and may, if we like, allow levity to creep in now and again, but he teaches us how we can improve ourselves if we think it worth while.

'Lying with his long Etonian legs on the sofa in a negligent, grown-up attitude.' Thus Gwen Raverat later described and drew her cousin, Bernard, in her book, 'Period Piece'. He is wearing a red flannel doll's cap given him on his fourteenth birthday by his other cousin in the picture, Frances.

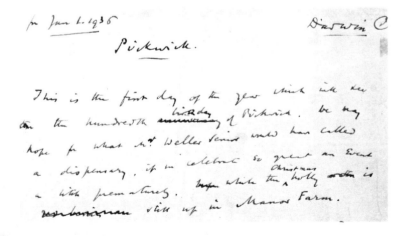

The opening paragraph of a manuscript article written in ink by Bernard Darwin for 'The Times' of 1 January 1936 for the hundredth anniversary of the first appearance of Pickwick. A typical Weller quotation emerges from the elusive handwriting.

A well-balanced finish to his swing, suggesting fluency and poise in spite of the buttoned jacket and cuff-linked shirt. Taken at Hoylake in 1921 when he reached the semi-finals of the Amateur championship for the second time.

His ungainly putting stance contrasts with the ease of his swing (above). The squares are six inches wide, which makes his toes almost four feet apart. The picture is taken from George Beldam's book, 'Great Golfers'.

On reaching the semi-finals of the Amateur championship in 1921, Darwin earned the distinction of featuring in a Tom Webster cartoon in the 'Daily Mail'. Three down at the turn against the last American left in the tournament, he won at the 19th.

Gene Sarazen, American and British Open champion, at Hoylake in 1956 on one of his return visits to the Open, talks to the man whose writings showed a profound admiration for the American's game.

Prize-fighting prints and a selection of his favourite books form the background to this picture of Darwin, taken in 1952.

1947. Outside the club-house of his beloved Rye, Darwin, as President of the Oxford and Cambridge Golfing Society, stands between the finalists in the Society's winter tournament (the President's Putter) who were (left) Leonard Crawley, who won by 3 and 2, and (right) P. B. 'Laddie' Lucas.

Ghastly, Horrible, but True (1929)

Miss Joyce Wethered beat Miss Glenna Collett in the final of the Ladies' championship at St Andrews by three holes up and one to play. Many epithets will be used to describe the fluctuations of the match and the quality of the play. I feel unequal to the effort and will let stark figures without adjectives speak. Miss Collett went out in 34 and was five up. She came home in 41 and was pulled down to two at luncheon. She went out in 42, lost six holes out of nine and was four down at the turn in the afternoon. She did the next eight holes in 36, including a seven, got one hole back and lost by three and one.

It was a great match, greatly played, and the statement that Miss Wethered played her game and yet was taken to the 35th hole is the highest compliment that could be paid to Miss Collett. Both played magnificently, and that before so big a crowd, well behaved, impartial, and amenable to the refining influence of women with the flag, but yet so big and so eager as to make the players' task a hard and exhausting one. I can only echo the words of a famous St Andrews golfer who stood by me in the crowd and murmured over and over again in dazed admiration; 'Wonderful how they can do it!' It was wonderful, and America can be every bit as proud of the lady champion who has come here and lost as she is of her various male champions who have come here and won.

As to Miss Wethered, if she prefers now once more to retire

into private golf she can do so with the knowledge that she has given as complete proof of surpassing greatness as any game player of either sex that ever lived.

It was grey, still, perfect golfing weather when the first round began. Miss Collett had the honour and outdrove Miss Wethered by a few yards. Incidentally there was very little in it in the point of length but what there was, perhaps five or six yards on the average, was in Miss Wethered's favour since, leaving out of account two short holes, Miss Collett played the odd ten times more than Miss Wethered in this first round.

A rather loose, wide approach by Miss Wethered followed by three putts gave Miss Collett the first hole. It was at the second, however, that things began to look a little ugly. Miss Collett was wide on the right with her second and ran her third several yards past the hole. Miss Wethered had a perfect second and seemed sure of her four but putted six feet short. The fates did not forgive her. Miss Collett banged in her curly putt, the ball running right round the tin before dropping. Miss Wethered missed and in place of all square England was two down. Miss Wethered revived our spirits with a lovely three at the 3rd, the third successive three she has had at this hole, and the 4th was halved in four. Then, just as we felt that all was well and would soon be better still, epoch-making events began to happen in an almost incredible manner.

Both were on the green in three at the Long hole; Miss Wethered putted first and overran the hole, Miss Collett holed a four- or five-yard putt for a four, and was two up again. The Heathery hole was halved, Miss Wethered only saving herself by the skin of her teeth, and next came the blackest half-hour of all. Miss Collett was caught in the nasty little pot bunker behind the High hole green; Miss Wethered was perfectly safe just off the green and ran up the odd to within four feet. That was tolerably cheerful but Miss Collett ploughed her ball splendidly out of the sand and holed another four-yarder. Miss Wethered who palpably had not got the touch of her putter missed in the like and that was three down.

Worse and still worse were to come. Miss Collett was only just on the 8th green with her tee shot but she holed a twenty-five yard putt for two. It was black magic, ghastly, horrible, but true. Miss Wethered made a noble attempt for a half and her ball stopped just the fraction of a millimetre short of the hole. At the 9th Miss Wethered was bunkered from the tee, played a lovely pitch out, had a four in her grasp and then putted dreadfully short and took six. Miss Collett made no mistake; that was 34 out and five up.

Never have I heard so grim a silence fall on a crowd since Mr Walter Travis was holing long putts against Mr Edward Blackwell at Sandwich in 1904. At the 10th a hole seemed sure to come back, for Miss Wethered played a great approach shot and from her putt the ball disappeared into the hole. Out it came again, however, through some malign influence, and Miss Collett got her four and a half. The 11th was halved in three; Miss Collett was still five up and had holed eleven holes in 41 shots without a single five. It was overwhelming golf worthy of any male champion. She seemed certain to be six up at the 12th where Miss Wethered was again terribly short and Miss Collett had only to hole from a yard to win, but she dragged the ball across the hole and missed. There came a sigh of relief from the crowd. Every man, woman and child felt that now was the time. The crisis was past and Miss Wethered was going to recover.

The change did not come at once, however, for Miss Wethered again putted very, very short at the Hole o' the Cross and had to hole a supremely gallant putt of four yards to save her neck. Then at last, at the Long hole, came a real gleam of sunshine. With one just over the green and one just short, it was Miss Wethered who got nearest in four, Miss Wethered who got her five. Down to four. At the 16th Miss Wethered was a little inside all the way. She had a five-foot putt to win and she put it in. Down to three. The Road hole was halved in five but at the last hole Miss Wethered again had the best of the putting. Going out Miss Collett had looked as though she could miss nothing; now she was human once more. She played the odd from five feet and missed; Miss

Wethered had her four-footer for the hole and everybody felt it was an intensely crucial putt. Two down in four meant better than three down. In it went and again there was a great sigh of relief, 'It's all right; she's got her now'. Such was the general verdict and some even added as the ball rang against the tin: 'That's the match.'

The afternoon round began with a greatly increased crowd and an almost overwhelming feeling of confidence in our own champion. Sure enough, everything went swimmingly. Miss Wethered was at her very best. Miss Collett never cracked or looked like cracking, but she was putting iron shots a little farther from the hole than in the morning, and she had become an ordinary, uninspired mortal on the greens. So the fours turned to fives and fives were no good here. Miss Wethered began by holing a six-yard putt for a win in three. The 2nd was halved in five and Miss Wethered had the inside turn all the way to the 3rd and squared. The same thing happened at the 4th and she was one up. Miss Collett came back at her bravely and holed a fine putt at the Long hole for her four after Miss Wethered had reached the green with two giant shots. The tide was however setting too strongly in Miss Wethered's favour and for a while Miss Collett could not fight it. She was bunkered with rather hooked tee shots at the Heathery and High holes and she took three putts at the 8th. Miss Wethered played all three holes perfectly and won them all, and then rubbed it in by laying her approach dead at the 9th for a three. Four up at the turn and all seemed over.

Little did we imagine we were yet to suffer tortures. Now was the time of Miss Collett's supremely courageous counter-attack. A fine pitch and a three-yard putt won her the 9th in three; she played a beauty to the 11th and Miss Wethered hooked into the Hill bunker. She won the hole in three to four and that was down to two. She saved herself with a good putt at the 12th but cut her second at the Hole o' the Cross and lost it. The counter-attack seemed to be definitely stopped. Three up with five to play was surely good enough. But no, the most agonizing time was to come. Both players after all this magnificent golf went suddenly and simultaneously mad for just one hole. They got into bunkers, they bolted for the hole and ran past; they laid stymies, they missed short putts, Miss Wethered missed the shortest and lost in eight against seven. The next moment both were sane again and playing as skilfully as ever. Miss Collett played the 15th perfectly; she lay stone dead in three. Miss Wethered pushed her drive, went a little short with her approach, and a little strong with her run-up. She lay five or six yards away and down to one stared her in the face. Then, heaven be praised, she hit that putt slap bang into the middle of the hole. It was hard on Miss Collett but it was a putt that deserved to win a championship and it settled this one. Miss Collett stuck to it splendidly but she had no more chances. The 16th was beautifully halved and that was dormy two. Each hit two admirable wooden club shots to the Road hole; each was a little too canny with the approach. It was about impossible to see what happened and every stroke seemed to take an eternity since the crowd had to be compressed and chaperoned before a shot could be played. At last a ball rolled up on the green and stayed ten feet short. Somebody tall enough to see said it was Miss Collett's. Another rolled up and lay eighteen inches from the hole. A mighty shout left no doubt that it was Miss Wethered's. Miss Collett tried for a three and missed, and a great match was over.

Not So Elementary (1953)

Some of the most famous and familiar sayings when run to earth in books of reference are found to bear the stigma of being 'attributed'. The Duke of Wellington's remark about the playing fields of Eton is, to say the least of it, suspect, and there seems little doubt that he never said 'Up, Guards, and at 'em', although in his own words he 'must have said and probably did say "Stand up, Guards" '. Regarding a more peaceful battlefield another and a bitter blow has lately fallen; George Hirst has broken all our hearts by declaring that he did not say 'Wilfred, we'll get them by singles'. He had pointed out that no batsman would thus deliberately deny himself the chance of a boundary, though we certainly have heard of Yorkshire doing so before lunch on the first day of the Lancashire match. Yet with all our cherished quotations being 'debunked' one by one we had held fast to 'Elementary, my dear Watson'. And now there comes along an inconoclastic and disenchanting gentleman (writing in the *Spectator*) who roundly asserts that Sherlock Holmes never used those words. What is worse, a hurried and imperfect search seems to show that he is right. 'My dear Watson' is easy; as the two men grew better acquainted it gradually superseded 'My dear Doctor'. The component parts of the desiderated phrase can nearly nearly but alas, not quite, be found together in 'The Crooked Man'. 'I have the advantage of knowing your habits, my dear Watson,' said Holmes and deduced that the practice justified a hansom. 'Excellent!' I cried. 'Elementary,' said he.

This exclamation of 'Excellent!' produced a particular reaction so nearly identical, that students capable of a decent second class might well fall into error. In 'The Reigate Squires' after a demonstration as to hand-writing, 'Excellent!' cried Mr Acton. 'But very superficial,' said Holmes. Again, in *A Study in Scarlet*, the earliest of all the writings, is the passage – 'Wonderful!' I ejaculated. 'Commonplace,' said Holmes. This is the best that can be made of a bad job on the spur of the moment. Heaven forbid that we should absolutely deny that those now almost sacred words can be discovered but they do not seem to be there. Holmes often used far more unkind expressions towards his friend as when (in 'The Sussex Vampire') he tartly observed in response to a suggestion 'We must not let him think this Agency is a home for the weakminded.' So too 'Good old Watson' implied a certain derision not to be found in 'My dear Watson'. But that peculiarly galling epithet 'elementary' appears to occur but once. It is a little sad; it would have been better, if the expression be permissible, to let sleeping attributions lie. And yet all but the most scholarly of us will soon get over the blow and will go on happily misquoting to the end of time.

Laughter on the Links (1934)

A small scene came suddenly back to me the other day with startling clearness. My kind tutor at Cambridge and his wife used every October term to go through a most painful martyrdom. In the course of the term they asked to dinner all his new pupils at the rate of five freshmen at a time. Further, since freshmen, however miserable they may be, can seldom pluck up courage to say 'Good-night' and go away, one third-year man was asked as well, both to perform this necessary function and generally to leaven the lump. On one occasion the proceedings became so lame and halting that our host and hostess introduced in despair the subject of a literary examination paper, in which one question related to famous bursts of laughter in literature. Amid a deathly silence I did my best by citing one from *Pendennis*, and afterwards one of the party was heard describing the evening with the utmost horror, and his voice rose almost to a scream as he said, 'There was one fellow there who actually answered a bit of one question!'

This has nothing to do with golf, but I was reminded of it by golf. At that solemn game it is not considered right to burst into laughter over our enemy's misfortunes, and I have often been gratefully aware of the heroic efforts of my opponents not to laugh at me. At the last weekend, however, I was playing in a team match by foursomes, and if it could not perhaps be said of the players that they were 'grand gowfers a', nane better', all of them could claim at least a reasonable degree of competence.

Nevertheless there arose in the course of the two days three separate occasions on which it seemed almost permissible to guffaw loudly.

The most remarkable of these instances was the halving of the last hole in seven strokes apiece. The story is so long that I can only tell parts of it. It was not a long hole, since it could be reached with a drive and a pitch, and it possessed a green of a type I do not like, having a back wall and two side walls. Parenthetically I do not like it because my own ball always seems to hover on the top of the wall and then drop over on the far side, whereas my opponent's, after a similar period of suspense, runs back and lies dead. A and B were dormy one on C and D, and both sides drove down the middle of the course. A played the odd, a shot which he described as 'quite good but not held up quite enough'; the ball fell over the right-hand side wall. C, determined to hold his shot up enough, hooked whole-heartedly. D, being convinced that A and B could not do worse than a five, tried to be clever and get a four; he was far too clever and failed to get over a bump.

The rest of the story of C and D's seven is a little shadowy, and I will return to A and B. B said it would be safest to putt over the wall. He putted with such good will that the ball climbed the first wall at full speed, ran the whole width of the green, and vanished over the wall on the other side. A said he would also putt, but putt more temperately. He did, and the ball came back to his feet. B had the third putt, and again the ball almost scaled the summit, but, alas! failed to do so by the material inch. Then exclaimed A, in the manner of Lady Macbeth:

'Infirm of purpose! Give me the daggers.'

He played the fourth putt, and a great one it was, for the ball just, and only just, got over the wall, trickled down the far side, and lay dead. C and D, after nameless adventures, had a putt for a six and missed it. So A and B kept their lead of one, and both sides left the green apoplectic with laughter.

The other two incidents were by comparison prosaic. In one case an eminent personage, who has played in a Walker Cup match, missed the globe in a bunker; his object was presumably to hit the sand, but all he did hit was the air, for the club passed high over the ball. In the other a most excellent player was required to play a short pitch and run to an open green. What he did play was an 'explosion' shot through the green. His club stuck in the turf some inches behind the ball, which spouted gently into the air and fell down not more than five feet from the spot whence it had started.

I can give no adequate explanation of these phenomena. I can only most solemnly assert that they occurred. Mr Snodgrass on a famous occasion explained that 'It was the salmon,' and perhaps this time it may have been the lobster. However that may be, I think that in each case a smile was allowable, and if the smile developed into a roar the victim had no right to be seriously annoyed. After all this match was not a championship, and I have heard of a player laughing at his enemy in a championship. It was that admirable and usually sedate golfer, the late Mr G. F. Smith, who once confessed as much to me. He was playing the 3rd hole at Prestwick, the Cardinal, in the days when the stone wall still existed at the back of the green. His opponent, having a difficult pitch to play, decided – and very wisely – to use the back wall, but his ball pitched on the wrong bump on that rather bumpy green and jumped lightly over the wall. Mr Smith sat down on the green and justifiably convulsed with laughter.

In the example from *Pendennis*, which I quoted at that nightmare dinner party, the Chevalier Strong 'had the grace not to laugh for five minutes, when he exploded into fits of hilarity'. Perhaps that is the kindest as well as the most discreet course. Many things may happen in five minutes, and even the missing of the globe may lose its sting if we hole a long putt immediately afterwards. Of course we who have missed the globe ought to start the laughter ourselves, and we shall be more likely to hole that compensating putt if we do, but there are some heights hard to attain, some walls we cannot putt over.

Pulling Hal's Leg (1949)

A far wider circle than that of the members of Deal golf club will think gratefully of Halford-Hewitt (Hal is what everyone called him) because he brought to the links there the tournament for the cup which bears his name. In the twenty-five years since he gave that cup, the tournament has become a wholly unique festival, unique in popularity, in the number of players it attracts, and in its own very special character, as at once a gigantic meeting of old friends and a contest of desperate school patriotism. It has grown and grown till it has now reached almost unwieldy proportions, and this year there were over fifty teams of ten players each, representing old boy golfing societies of the public schools.

The tournament began in 1924 with a comparatively modest number of entries. The matches were played on a variety of courses and at intervals. It was good and exciting fun enough, and we all wanted to win, but it was hard work for them who had to do the collecting of the teams, and it dragged on perhaps just a little too long. Then in the following year came the happy notion of playing the whole tournament off at Deal. From that moment the real fun began; the Deal week-end, for it was at first little more than a week-end, became something eagerly to look forward to, and the tournament's success became ever greater. It is certain that nobody looked forward to it more enthusiastically than did Hal himself, and no doubt it added if possible to his happiness that his own school of Charterhouse should have to their credit such a long series of victories. Hal was a frank and splendid partisan; he adored his Carthusians and suffered tortures of anxieties, though he pretended not to, over their fortunes. Indeed he suffered far more than they ever did, for they have always played in a fine light-hearted spirit. At the same time he was always the best and most gracious of losers, ready with wholly sincere congratulations to any other school that had the hardihood to win.

I have many visions of him in the course of the play. He did not often go far afield, but hung about the 17th or 18th greens watching the finishes and waiting anxiously for news. As he grew older and his health more frail, his particular watch-tower was in the big plate-glass window of the upper room of the club-house. Thither his friends would repair to give him the latest news from the Carthusian front. It was a rather noisy performance for Hal grew very deaf so that we had to shout our intelligence to him and he in turn would shout loudly back.

Sometimes his own side, who treated him with an affectionate lack of respect, would play unkindly on his emotions, and I have a particular recollection of John Morrison coming complete with a very long face to yell at him quite fictitious news of disaster. For a moment or two Hal looked thoroughly depressed, then he pulled himself together to make the best of it and reiterate his confidence in the recuperative powers of his team; finally he would realise that his patriotic leg was being pulled and would break into a loud laugh of relief, while pouring friendly abuse on the deceiver's head. As regards that particular informant he grew in time more wary, but he was always liable to sudden shocks from others, if they had the heart to administer them, and indeed, I think, rather enjoyed them than otherwise, as forming part of a tradition.

It was sad that for the last two years he was not well enough to come to Deal. It would have been palpably too exhausting for him but it was hard work to keep him away. This year when he heard that his Carthusians were once more in the final, relays of his friends had to go to the telephone to try to dissuade him from his project of driving all the way from his home in Suffolk to see the battle. I was called, among others, to talk to him, as being an impartial person with no talent for leg-pulling, who could give him an objective view. I told him I thought his side would win, as in fact they did, but for a moment I felt I had been unwise, for he was the more eager to come. However, and it does not lie heavy on my conscience, I also told him, as did others, that there was a strong, cold wind blowing at Deal which had a restraining effect. He then asked whether I thought that a little champagne would be good for the side on the eve of the final. And to this I was able to give an unqualified assent. What the Carthusians would have done to me had I said otherwise I shudder to think.

Slow Cobs at Downe (1941)

Some few summers ago Watt, the Kent fast bowler who comes from Westerham, kindly brought a team to play against our village on a Sunday for the benefit of a local charity. All Downe rang with it and rumour declared that the whole Kent eleven and above all Woolley were coming.

> 'Town and Tower and Village
> Had heard the trumpet blast.'

and we drew reinforcements that would certainly be needed from all around. On the great day there was a ring encircling the field such as even old Nyren might not have disdained. Many of the 'grand old Kent eleven' did come, and in the middle of trouncing Middlesex, which made it all the better. Not Woolley, but one cannot have everything. Fagg who had been making hundred after hundred, Bryan, Chalk, Watt, Lewis, Sunnucks – have I left any out? At any rate that was stunning enough. Downe made some runs, not a great many but not cruelly few. The visitors were not too hard on us for Watt bowled far below his normal pace and Fagg's bowling reminded me of that of Tom Brown in the Marylebone match at Rugby, when he bowled 'slow cobs' to old Mr Aislabie. I am not precisely aware what these may be, but Fagg's bowling seemed to answer the description.

When our visitors went in, any well brought-up reporter could only have begun his account in one way. 'The start,' he would have written, 'was sensational'. The very first ball was a half volley to leg and Sunnucks lashed it manfully and was caught high up, a really magnificent catch by long-leg, running as if the devil was after him. Fagg made a few runs and then was caught off a mis-hit. This was all very well, but patriotism has its limits and we did not want to see all our distinguished guests get out thus quickly. We need not have been anxious. In came Chalk. Our hitherto successful bowler knew vaguely that he was a hitter and conceived the notion of keeping him quiet by bowling rather short. The result must have disappointed him because ball after ball was hooked out of the ground over the people, over the hedge and into the high road. After a delirious quarter of an hour of this sort of thing Chalk took to running out and the bowlers became so terrified that they could scarcely deliver the ball. He ran farther and farther down the pitch in valiant attempts to get out and once or twice he missed the ball, but our wicket-keeper was paralysed with anxiety and could do no more than juggle with it. All things come to an end; at last the wicket-keeper caught the ball, and this time he made sure; he swept all three stumps out of the ground with a triumphant gesture. The next year Ames came and made as many runs and quite as fast but I was away and did not see him: so the memory of Chalk's innings is enshrined without a rival in my heart.

Village cricket can vary in an extraordinary degree. In Hampshire, for instance, the original home of the noble game, there is that tiniest of villages Ovington. There, though one would hardly have supposed that the village could produce eleven men, the cricket would I fear put Downe to shame, possibly because it is played on a really good wicket in the park. Not only does the whole eleven turn out *cap-à-pie* in spotless flannels, equipped 'to the last gaiter-button', but some of the play is of a high order. I watched the gardener's son, as my reporter would say, 'compile a faultless century'. Here moreover was no raw-boned yokel 'with an arm as long as a hop pole', such as he who thrashed the great Lumpy's bowling all over the field 'in the most ludicrous manner' to the malicious delight of old Nyren. He was a polished batsman with the straightest of bats and never a touch of rusticity about him.

On the other hand on the only occasion I ever played for Aberdovey – it is forty years ago now – I thought the cricket less good. This was not in the summer holidays when there were sometimes great men among us; the famous Jimmy Douglas played once and the opposing umpire was ready to give him out at sight, but, before he had identified him, the champion was caught where no fielder ought to have been. My match was out of the holiday season and so we depended entirely on local talent. The conditions were, to be sure, difficult. After two hours of torrential rain we went straight out to play on a wicket consisting largely of slate. Our total was, I think, 38 and I will not conceal the fact that my eight, made against a poacher at one end and an organist at the other, was top score. Our total was not big enough to win but it nearly was, for Machynlleth, a town against a village, All Muggleton against poor Dingley Dell, made but little over 40. To-day, as far as I know, Aberdovey has an eleven no longer, but its next-door neighbour Towyn has and of Towyn cricket I desire to speak with all respect. It must be very hard to make runs there, for grass in the not very long field arrests the ball's progress without human intervention. I really mention Towyn to tell a small story of dear Mrs Foster, the mother of all the Fosters. A year or two since her eldest son, H.K., took her to watch a match there. Scarcely had she entered the ground when her eagle eye detected something amiss. 'There are,' she said, 'twelve men in the field.'

There is an enchanted village match in Sussex which belongs to another chapter and I pass on to a little cricket in the Cotswolds. Our team, if I may so term it, represents no mere single village; no less than four of them send their picked men to its ranks and on the banner which floats over its wooden shed are blazoned the letters V.C.C. – the Valley Cricket Club. It is one of the defects of living in a valley that the sides of it are steep and hence it is difficult to get a field well adapted to cricket. There is nothing amiss with the actual pitch, which is on a narrow flat ledge. It is religiously guarded from cattle by posts and rails and the pulling up of the posts on the morning of a match brings joy and interest to all the small boy population. Unfortunately, however, the ground falls away sharply on the farther side of the pitch so that, as the spectator comes through the gate, he sees some of the fielders cut off suddenly at the waist like a disappearing lady in a conjurer's trick. A ball hit on that side of the wicket might go for ten as did one of Noah Mann's down the slope of Windmill Down. That is, it might were it not for the hay, which is often luxuriant.

It is a sad day when the Valley are away rather than at home or when, as must too often happen in war time, the match has to be scratched. There is scarcely a pleasanter spot in the world from which to watch cricket than under the grey stone wall, well sheltered from the wind, looking over the ground to the other side of the valley, while the passing clouds trail their shadows across it. There are no smarter caps than those of scarlet and white in quarters which are the Valley's uniform, and no such beautiful embroidered braces anywhere as those that go with the caps. Here at least are retained the fashions of Pilch and Lillywhite and Alfred Mynn who did not disdain to play in braces. Alas! in war time there are few of these uniformed stalwarts and the gaps have to be filled by volunteers in blue jerseys. The Valley cricket is temporarily not quite what it was, but I shall always be grateful for one visiting batsman whom I saw play there. He was a member of a military eleven quartered temporarily in the neighbourhood, who came swirling through our narrow, muddy gateway in Army lorries and leaped out in full battle dress. He had a cheerful, devil-may-care air, a mop of yellow locks that bounced as he ran, and his braces were cleared for action, hanging loose about his loins. I christened him in my own mind the circular batsman because his methods showed a purely circular conception of the cricket stroke. A famous old St Andrews golfer, twice Open champion, Bob Martin, used to say, 'I drive like an auld wife cutting hay', and those words give a faint picture of my batsman's style. Nay, it was more than a style; it was clearly a fixed principle, a faith. The moment the ball left the bowler's hand, no matter whether it was fast or slow, short or well-pitched up, the circular batsman swung himself and his bat across the line of its flight, pivoting upon his left heel. What was more, if he missed the ball as he often did, he completed his swing and having made an entire turn, ended as he had begun facing the bowler. It was the method rather of a hammer thrower than a cricketer. It was for that ponderous and Olympic role that nature had clearly intended him; yet he several times struck the ball in the course of his revolutions, though his eye can never by any chance have seen it. He struck it to the value of some eight runs and nothing in his innings became him like the ending of it. He spun round like a teetotum, hit the ball as it passed him on the leg side, sent a high catch to short slip and simultaneously trod upon his wicket.

On the Way to the Grand Slam (1930)

The most remarkable thing about Mr Jones seems to me to be this, that he can win an Open championship without playing really well. He has now won this championship on each of his last three visits here. When he won it at St Andrews he was brilliant, and even he would have admitted that he was playing well. But both at St Annes and at Hoylake he was comparatively speaking struggling, and yet he could win. Of course we expect more of him than of anybody else and set in our minds an almost impossibly high standard. One man, as we know, may steal a horse and another may not look over the hedge. Well, poor Bobby may not go even anywhere near a hedge without our accusing him of a monstrous hook or an astounding slice. He certainly has a hard time of it from the critics of whom he himself is the most merciless of all.

Still, I must stick to it that at Hoylake, though he won the championship and was only three over a level of fours for four rounds of that tremendous course, he was by no means his best self. One always contemplated the possibility, however remote, of his playing a bad shot and when he is at his best a bad shot appears wholly impossible.

Bobby had no great confidence in any of his clubs at Hoylake except his putter and nobly did his putter justify it. He seemed to me to be distinctly unlucky with his putts and yet I imagine he took as few of them as any man in the competition, and further, saved himself untold anxiety by laying the long ones so close to the hole that the next became quite unmissable. He is so dazzling a player of the other shots that the watcher as a rule takes some little time to appreciate what a magnificent putter he is. His putting is apt to escape notice and so, at first, is his supreme mastery of the little chip from off the green. There never was such a man, unless it be Walter Hagen, for taking two shots when it might have been three. Those little shots from off the green, he says in *Down the Fairway*, 'they are the least spectacular in golf, I suppose, and the greatest stroke-savers if they are working for you'. Certainly they were working for him at Hoylake. Time and again he put them near the hole and then down went the putt with no bother or fuss or agonizing over the line – and as clean as a whistle. He never seemed to be doing, for him, particularly well and yet he was clinging to fours. Saving is less dramatic than gaining but a stroke saved is a stroke gained.

In the Amateur championship at St Andrews it was the wonderful consistency of his driving which more than anything else made Bobby win. At Hoylake it was his putting, and I think it is his putting which to a great extent accounts for the wonderful consistency of Bobby's record. Take the names of the really outstanding golfers in our history who can beyond question be called great golfers, and see how many of them could possibly be called great putters. I think you will find very few. Some are pretty good putters and some were on occasions downright bad ones, but these two Americans who have almost monopolised our championship in late years – Hagen and Bobby Jones – are both magnificent putters. There were many dramatic moments during the three crowded days at Hoylake but there is one that stands out in my mind above all others. It was in the third round when Bobby, after his usual bad start (those first three holes frightened him out of his life) had as usual retrieved himself and had brought his score back to under an average of fours. Then he had taken a five to the 14th and just about that moment violent outbursts of cheering began to come from Compston's crowds five holes behind. We knew that Compston had made a brilliant start and then had taken a six. Now he was evidently doing something brilliant again. Bobby began to take fives and with each five there synchronised another defiant yell from the rear which told of another three for Compston. Jones was dropping strokes and Compston was gaining them, and just about the time when the one had four fives in a row, the other was starting home 3, 3, 3, 2. As Bobby holed out his last putt for a 74 a spectator came flying across from the 14th green gasping out the news that Compston was seven under fours. Having had much experience of golfing lies I did not at first believe it, but it turned out to be true. England might lead by as many as three shots with one round to go. She did not since Compston took a six at the Dun and small blame to him, for he must have felt dizzy after all those threes. But she did lead by one. Compston's 68, coming when it did, was as fine an effort as ever was made in a championship. I suppose it took too much out of him for his afternoon round was a tragic collapse about which no more need be said. He had at any rate enjoyed one supreme golfing moment in the morning.

Diegel and Macdonald Smith tied for second place and Horton Smith was on their heels, but I will leave them unsung and turn to our native players again. Robson did wonderfully well, and allowing myself a few 'ifs and ans' which is an amiable weakness he might have done better still. He might even have won. He has been said to have missed seven putts of two feet each in a single round. That I believe to be nonsense. Lookers-on always exaggerate the shortness of putts. I saw one or two that Robson missed and they were more than two feet. They were undoubtedly short and he missed far too many of them. Up to that third round he had been putting beautifully and through the championship he played very well up to the pin. Every single soul in Hoylake would have liked to see him win. Confound that putting.

Cotton was in one sense disappointing as he raised such high hopes with his splendid first round of 70, yet he had a score of under 300, and it must be remembered that he had only just recovered from his illness and had a sore wrist into the bargain. Considering that he began the last day with a rather crushing seven, he did uncommonly well, and his fourth round of 73 represented a good honest determination to stick to it. He seemed to me a better player than he had ever been before. He is still very young and I think his time will come.

When Slices Were Slices (1935)

'That man, Sir,' said Mr Smangle, 'has comic powers that would do honour to Drury Lane Theatre. Hear him come the four cats in the wheelbarrow – four distinct cats, Sir, I pledge you my honour. Now you know that's infernal clever!'

Doubtless it was and still would be, but it is scarcely comparable with the cleverness of one who can 'come' six distinct kinds of slice. Such a man exists for I have just been reading his book, and a very good book too, *Standardised Golf Instruction*, by Seymour Dunn, descendant of a famous race of Musselburgh golfers and now a well-known teacher of golf in America. He defines each one of the six slices, describing the flight of the ball in language simple, but poignant; then he analyses the cause, tells the slicer which particular and fundamental rule he has violated, and finally he indicates the appropriate remedy. People have a habit of saying: 'What can one do to cure a slice?' and I have hitherto answered, as I believed truthfully: 'Nobody could tell you that without seeing you play.' Well, here is somebody who apparently can, and I take off my hat to him, being careful to do so in a graceful curve 'from the inside out'.

I do not propose to set out the six varieties of slice, though by now I have probably suffered from all of them. If I have not I feel as if I have, because to read a medical book is invariably to believe that one has got every disease under the sun; the reader goes about kicking his toe against the ground to make sure that it hurts him, as did Private Mulvaney in that terribly fine story 'Love o' Women'. Mr Dunn has, however, made me think with mingled horror and affection of the slices of yester year, and I have convinced myself that the modern golfer knows nothing of slicing. In the first place he has not got a gutty ball to be a plaything for the winds, and in the second, he has got a steelshafted club which does much to mitigate that ruthless curve of the ball to the right. An old friend of mine, now long since dead, on receiving some form of patent club, wrote to the maker: 'Thank you very much for your club; it has added fifty yards to my slice'. To say so much of a modern club would be unmeaning flattery. Let the youthful hooker believe me or believe me not, there were slicers in those days.

Who, for example, could rival the feats of one golfer of my acquaintance? He lived inglorious, a mere schoolmaster; he was not a great player and would be reckoned today a contemptibly short hitter; yet at eight holes out of the first nine at Aberdovey (the course was not then quite as it is now) he sliced his ball from the tee on to the railway line and in one instance – this is but incidental – the ball was carried in a passing train to Glandovey Junction, where it presumably changed for Borth and Aberystwyth. Over the sandy crest of Cader, over the 16th green, over the rushes and over the 'leeks' his ball soared and curved in a noble arc to find its appointed end. He 'hath not left his peer'.

Is there any man alive who could with the far-flying rubber-core do such a deed today? Of course there is not. Golfers are in this matter of slicing a decadent race. There is still flourishing a very good golfer who claims – and I have no doubt justly – to have hit the ball out of bounds at some time or other from every teeing ground at Hoylake, save only at the Rushes hole. That was, to be sure, not all done by slicing; indeed, he favours rather the low and smothered hook; but slicing must have played a not ignoble part in his achievement, and that achievement will never again be equalled.

For myself I am one of the rank and file of slicers; I cannot claim any such records as these, and yet I have memories once horrible, now through the passing of the years almost beautiful. There was a whole week once at Westward Ho! in which the wind blew great guns and never ceased from blowing. In that week I rose almost to the heights. I do not believe that my slice during those never-to-be-forgotten days was any one of Mr Dunn's six varieties. His description generally begins as follows: 'The ball starts out straight and continues to fly straight, but after two-thirds of its journey ...' My recollection is that my ball never even started straight, and certainly long before one-third of its strength was spent it was heading for the spiky and venomous rushes far to the right.

Neither do I believe that any one of his six causes can have accounted for a display so splendid in its ignominy. It may well be that 'centrifugal force generated by the swing was pulling the player off balance towards the ball', but that alone would never have accounted for it; I must have been violating all the 'fundamentals' at once – 'and then some'.

Let me not be deemed an inveterate praiser of the past who will not allow their puny triumphs to more modern golfers. With a ball which goes so much farther, if only they lose control over it sufficiently, they are not altogether impotent. I recall two fine feats at Rye by two distinguished Oxford golfers. One of them pitched his ball over the road and the railings when on the way, as he imagined, to the 7th hole; the other drove nearly into the road when going to the 16th.

It is doubtful, however, whether this second achievement ought to be reckoned as a slice; it was rather in the nature of a push, which according to Mr Dunn means merely a 'misdirection of the ball to the right'. This ball was certainly misdirected, but, as I remember it, it had no curl; it just proceeded in a bee-line over cover-point's head for the whole of its immense journey. I am afraid that shot must be disqualified; it lacked the essential point of the true and glorious slice. 'Definition of slice 4. The ball starts out to the left of the intended line of play and then swerves to the right' – that is the real thing.

A Secret Kingdom (1955)

All children have, I suppose, a secret kingdom of pretending, peopled by creatures of their own imagination, whose names and even existences are never revealed to the grown-up world. The Brontës, as we know, filled up many little books with endless stories of the princes and politicians in a country of their own. My creatures can make no such claim to such intellectual stature, but I do sometimes wonder whether any other small boy ruled so large an empire of game players and athletes, all possessed of names devised for them on their creator's private principle. Their names were founded entirely on those of dogs, cats or horses belonging to the family, its sisters, cousins, aunts or friends. What may be called the two main root names were those of Otter, a beloved and tangled mongrel whose ancestry defied analysis, and the Brom Cat, who deserves a word of explanation. A half-German cousin came to stay; she possessed little English conversation but when she had nothing else to say she declared that our cat purred, 'Sie Brummt'. For some reason I seem to have spelt her with an 'o' instead of a 'u'. To those root names, as to a number of others, were added terminations – brook, ford, and so forth, also prefixes such as Mac and Fitz. Otter, for instance, gave first of all the name of the chief county, Otterhive, and that is a termination for which I cannot now account. The capital was Otterville, in Otterfordshire, and so on. The Brom Cat produced Bromsland – a Scotland as opposed to an England – Brombridge,

Bromcombe and Brommanoir. This was clearly founded on
Beaumanoir, the formidable old person in *Ivanhoe* who was the
ruler of Templestowe.

Does the reader think I am going mad or am merely a bore? It is
hard for me to tell because these doubtless absurd names seem so
entirely natural and commonplace to me that I cannot judge of
their effect on others. I think that I began to create them when I
was eight or nine and I certainly went on till I was fourteen and at
Eton. If I write nostalgically about them I do not wish to be
thought a pathetic and lonely little boy who had to people his
solitude with these strange companions. My family, if they had
not my passion for the public and heroic figures in games, were
quite as fond of games themselves in a reasonable way. They were
perhaps a little surprised at the violence of my feelings, even as
they were at my taste, evinced for a very brief season, for going to
church; but they were certainly not unsympathetic. If I did not
tell them about my secret empire, it was not for fear of being a
bore but because I had no desire to share it with anybody. Quite
the reverse indeed; it was something to hug to oneself; its name
was not to be spoken.

Of course I have forgotten a good deal but I have remembered
much. Just as a test I have tried to recite the Donlandshire cricket
eleven (Don was somebody's dog and had a popular root name),
and I have written down nine of them. There is no crib extant, but
I know I am right. Even though they were the champion county
and came from the North, at once so sinister and so romantic, that
is not bad after sixty something years. I could not do as much for
any real county eleven of today. The wicket-keeper has escaped
me but there were two Donlands, one of them Sir Richard, two
Druidthorpes (J. A. and P. F.), Ottercliffe (J. W.), Brancliffe, a
really tremendous all-rounder, Otterpool, fast right, Tossbrook,
slow left-hand, and Brommanoir aforesaid.

I set out their names as they illustrate the principle. Don, as I
said, was a dog; Druid a very ancient carriage horse of my grandmother's. Bran, another dog, a greyhound so early in family
history that only his name remained; Toss, an ill-tempered collie

belonging to cousins. Dogs certainly predominated, though there were at least two cats, Tina and Jerry. Dick was very popular, being my grandmother's shrill fox terrier. Dickingham Parish Church, for example, was a Rugby Football team (in red and white stripes), the name of which still sounds stirring; Ottercliffe and the two Druidthorpes both played for it during the winter season. Somebody had a small, odious pet called Flirt, and even she was pressed into the service. Does C. H. Flirtingale sound a likely or even a respectable name for a football player? I suppose not but, as I said, I am quite incapable of judging. In a few cases animals who had no real claim were allowed to creep in. There were Toutou and Trotineau, small animals made I think of cotton-wool, resident on the chimney-piece and called after some creatures in a French story-book. Le Toutou was a highly distinguished all-rounder (cricket and rugby), and Chateautrotineau (P. C.) was not to be despised. I have lately discovered from a copy-book, which had not been seen for fifty years at least, that he was also a weight-putter.

It cannot be denied that Otterhive was a county of all-rounders. Names had to be provided for cricketers, football players of both codes, runners, jumpers, and golfers. This was a great tax on the invention and besides it was more exciting to have personages who excelled in anything they attempted. It was before the days of C. B. Fry, but there were others such as Stoddart, and I had dimly heard of Alfred Lyttelton as a universal genius. So I distinctly remember that P. F. Druidthorpe, before mentioned, batted for Otterhive, left-handed beyond doubt, was a fine Rugby forward, his brother being the three-quarter, and jumped 6 ft 2½ ins.

It must not be thought that these men played purely on paper or in their creator's imagination. They did their best to play in real life but it was difficult, for there could be but one impersonator, myself. To take anyone else into my confidence, I am sure, never occurred to me. Only I knew who I was; to the cold world I appeared to be merely a small boy playing by himself on the lawn. Cricket consisted in bowling practice, generally indoors, in particular down the long passage at Down House with the vermilion fire-engine as a wicket. Association football was like-wise played as a rule indoors with a lawn tennis ball in the hall of my grandmother's house at Cambridge. I recall the crash of a goal scored against the front door. It must have made life hard to bear for everybody else in the house. Rugby, on the other hand, was played out of doors. I possessed a Rugby ball which I passed from hand to hand in brilliant combined runs down the lawn till at last it was triumphantly grounded by the corner-flag under the branches of the big plane tree. That to be sure did put a certain strain on the powers of make-believe, but it was otherwise with the attempt at goal which followed the try. A kind gardener had made me two sets of miniature Rugby posts, complete with cross-bar, and it was no easy matter to kick a goal from the touch-line. That was emphatically the real agonising thing. Even the easy one straight in front of the posts, after one had rounded the enemy full-back and buried one's shoulder in the muddy grass, was not without its anxieties.

Golf would obviously seem to have lent itself best of all to my solitary ritual, but though there were some famous players such as Mactina and Toutouburn, both clearly from Bromsland, which was Scotland, I think they played but little; at any rate they could not compare in splendour with the cricketers. I fancy that was because golf was too real, and too earnest. If I did a heavenly two at the hole where one lofted over the box trees and I once pitched the ball on my sister Frances's nose as she stood at the flag, that two was too precious to be allotted to any imaginary person-age. Of course it would have been a one if my sister had not put her nose in the way. Golf was too serious for pretending.

I have kept to the end my last discovery; it is an old copy-book, used from internal evidence, at different dates, for it contains some French lessons, a list of inn signs round Cambridge, an essay on the best way of arranging stamps, the 'History of the World (with notes), by B. R. M. Darwin', which seems never to have gone any further. There is also a good deal of 'B.R.M.D.' (scribbled here and there, for even heroic initials are not quite so

141

fascinating as one's own). And then at the end there is a series of letters beginning 'Dear Sir', written to the various people who have been selected to play for Otterhive, telling them of this agreeable honour and asking for an immediate reply. There is a grandeur of pretending about this that compels my own admiration. The thing was carried through with such thoroughness.

And with that I must say a reluctant goodbye to all those good companions, or rather *au revoir*, for I can always call them up to haunt me pleasantly whenever I like. I feel like the Reverend John Mitford as he said farewell to the great Hambledon eleven. 'Unwillingly,' he said, 'do we drop the pen. Very pleasant has our task been, delightful our recollections. Farewell ye thymey pastures of our beloved Hampshire and farewell ye spirits of the brave who still hover over the fields of your inheritance.' It is oftenest over my grandmother's garden at Cambridge that the spirits of my brave will hover. I can see it all with extraordinary clearness, the goal-posts between the big beech and the plane at one end and against the box trees at the other. The flower-beds and the gravel walk on either side, representing touch, and on the path Mr Bourne who kindly made my posts, the most unresting of all gardeners, in a hat like Sir Winston Churchill's, comes walking as if the devil were after him. Dicky's piercing bark is heard heralding my grandmother in her Bath chair and for a moment I must restrain that deft punt to touch – into the veranda. No matter, the Parish Church three-quarters must score in the end. There they go, they have scored under the sweeping branches of the plane tree, I knew they would; nothing can stop them. They come from Donlandshire.

Harry Vardon (1937)

Comparison between players of different generations are, as a rule, futile, and particularly so in the case of golf, since the conditions under which it is played have so greatly changed; but no one who ever saw Vardon in his best days can doubt that his genius was unsurpassable. Those days are now rather distant because, although he won the last of his six Open championships in 1914, it was at the end of the nineteenth and the beginning of the twentieth century that he was in his most glorious prime. When he won the third of his championships in 1899 no one so much as dreamed that there could be another champion. He went up and down the country winning tournaments and breaking records, trampling down all opponents in his juggernaut stride. He did what only a very great player can do; he raised the general conception of what was possible in his game and forced his nearest rivals to attain a higher standard by attempting that which they would otherwise have deemed impossible. He had a great influence, too, on methods of playing. When he first appeared his notably upright swing, though so full of grace and rhythm, came as a shock to the orthodoxy of the time, but has now long since been accepted.

Three of his six championships were won after the introduction of the rubber-cored ball in 1902, but it was with the gutty, before his serious illness, that he was supreme. Had it not been for that breakdown in health his tally of victories would surely have been much longer; it was after his illness that his putting began to betray him. The modern golfer believes that Vardon was always a bad putter, but this is not so. He was not an outstanding putter, nor had he quite the same graceful ease on the green as elsewhere, but he was at least a very good approach putter and a competent holer-out. He could never otherwise have accomplished half of what he did.

Vardon's record is so long that it must be severely compressed. He was born on 9 May 1870, at Grouville in Jersey. He learnt the game there as a caddie and continued to play after starting work as a gardener at the age of thirteen. His younger brother, Tom, was the first to go out into the world, as assistant professional at St Annes, and it was he who induced Harry to apply for a post at Ripon in 1890. In 1891 he moved to Bury in Lancashire and thence to Ganton in 1896. He had first played in the Open championship at Prestwick in 1893 (the year of Taylor's debut), but it was at Ganton that he became famous. In the spring of 1896 Taylor, who had been two years champion, came there to play Vardon a match and went home defeated by 8 and 6 and full of his conqueror's praises. A month or two later they tied for the Open championship at Muirfield and Vardon won the play-off by three strokes. In 1897 he fell away slightly, but won again at Prestwick in 1898 and the following year won with perfect ease at Sandwich. These were his two supreme years. It was in 1899 that he beat Taylor, who was playing well, by 11 and 10 in the final of the tournament at Newcastle, County Down, and also beat Willie Park in one of the outstanding matches of his life.

In 1900 Vardon set out on what was practically a year's tour of the United States, though he broke it to come home to defend his title in the championship and finished second to Taylor at St Andrews. In America, where golf was still young, he travelled from end to end of the country playing an enormous number of matches and causing great enthusiasm; he hardly lost a match and won the American championship.

But the hard work of the tour took its toll, and it is doubtful if he was ever so brilliant again. After being twice runner-up in the championship to Braid and Herd respectively, he won at Prestwick in 1903 with a total of 300, and this he regarded as the best of all his achievements, since he was so unwell that he nearly fainted several times in his last round. Soon afterwards he had to spend some time in a sanatorium and made a more or less complete recovery. In 1905 came the second great match of his career, in which he and Taylor beat Braid and Herd over four greens by 11 and 10. Their play at Troon, where they won fourteen holes, was astonishingly fine, and so it was on the last links, Deal, though Vardon had had a haemorrhage the night before and was not really fit to play at all.

There followed a period of comparatively lean years and then, to the general joy, Vardon won again at Sandwich, in 1911, beating Massy so convincingly in playing off the tie that the great French player gave up at the 35th hole. The year 1913 saw Vardon tie for yet another Open championship, that of the United States, at The Country Club at Brookline. This was the historic occasion on which Mr Francis Ouimet, then little older than a schoolboy, beat Vardon and Ray after a triple tie and may be said to have founded the American golfing empire. It was unquestionably a disappointing blow for Vardon; yet he won his sixth championship next year at Prestwick, beating Taylor by three shots. The two were drawn together on the last day and took the whole of a rather obstreperous crowd with them so that it was a marvel that they could play as they did.

When the war was over Vardon was almost fifty and his victorious days were of necessity nearly over. Yet in 1920 he tied for second place in the American championship, one stroke behind Ray. In all human probability he would have won had not a fierce wind come up as he was playing the last few holes and was tiring fast. That was his final achievement, and during the later years of his life his health put golf to all intents and purposes out of the question. He bore the deprivation with philosophy and sweet temper, enjoying teaching when he could not play and always anxious to watch the younger players. This he did with an eye at once kindly and critical, being a staunch conservative and unshaken in his conviction that the greatest qualities of the game had departed with the gutty ball. From 1903 to the end of his life he was professional to the South Herts Golf Club at Totteridge, where he was an oracle and an institution. He has left a name affectionately regarded by everyone and an ineffaceable mark on the game of golf.

Paralysis that Passes (1936)

In watching the play in the *Golf Illustrated* Gold Vase at the Berkshire Club, it was interesting to notice how the little additional pace of the greens troubled a good many of the competitors. They were not really very fast, but they were faster than those to which the players had lately been accustomed, and so every now and again one saw an eminent person run his ball clean out of holing distance and hold up his hands to high heaven in bewilderment. No one complained; everybody honestly allowed that the greens were admirable; it was just that little unexpected fire in them that was, for a while, so puzzling.

To my mind, a good golfer may say that the greens are too slow for him; he ought very, very seldom to say positively that they are too fast. Those who commit themselves to this general statement are, as a rule, not good golfers. A friend of mine, the moving spirit of a golf club, received the other day a solemn complaint that the greens were too fast. It was couched in terms such as are more used in praise than blame, for the complainant described the greens as being 'like billiard tables'. It was an unintentional compliment which, in my experience, they fully deserve.

My friend answered him with the utmost tact, and yet with a proper pride. He pointed out that in March greenkeepers were more concerned with lack of growth than with cutting, but had to 'run over' the greens occasionally; that on the day in question there had been a period of three weeks with hardly any rain, and that during that time the wind had been mainly from the east and south-east. He added that when the season's growth came the greens would not be really fast, but – and I like this little touch of defiance – 'I am glad to say they are seldom slow'.

To that I can only add 'Hooroar for the principle'; but, then, I confess to thinking that putting is only worthy of the name on a reasonably fast green. It is a skilful enough business, no doubt, on slow ones and requires a certain bulldog courage, but the poetry and beauty are gone out of it. It is always pleasanter to hole putts than to miss them, and to hole them on the slowest greens is good hostile fun, for it annoys the enemy and wins the half-crowns, but there is surely no comparison in point of ecstasy between the soothing and the bludgeoning of the ball into the hole.

The Americans speak of a player 'stroking' a ball well on the green. They use the word, I am afraid, to mean that he has a good putting stroke, and in that sense I take leave to dislike it, to class it with 'glimpsing' and 'savouring'. If it be used in the sense of caressing, then it conveys the perfect description of the perfect putt, but only on a fast green. Golf 'hath not anything to show more fair' than a good putter, for preference with a club of wood, playing a long putt on a big green; striking the ball so gently that everybody gives a gasp, as if to say 'He's short'; so truly that the ball comes on and on, to rest six inches beyond the hole or haply to drop in.

Let me take an extreme case. The green of the High hole coming in at St Andrews is sometimes admittedly too fast, but on the days when it is not, when the ball can just be made to stop and no more, is there any sensation equal to that of laying the putt dead from the very brink of the Eden? The ball goes winding on its way down and across the slope; it seems now and then almost to stop, now and then fatally to gather speed; at last it nestles so close to the hole – and it must be very close on that green – that we are given the next one. That seems to me to be putting in its fullness, when up to the very last moment we are not sure whether the ball will lie stone dead or, with a horrid little spurt when at its last gasp, run four feet past. And, as to the man who can keep the touch of his club in such conditions, I say, with Locksley, 'I call him an archer fit to bear bow and quiver before a king, an it were the stout King Richard himself'.

Pace is relative. I have a vivid recollection of playing cricket during the War, after an interval of many years, on a wicket of cast-iron, sunburnt ground, covered by a strip of material technically known as 'covers waterproof green 30×30'. For the first four balls of the first over from a bowler by no means in the 'body-line' class, I had not moved my bat from the block by the time the ball was in the wicket-keeper's hands. Quite unintentionally I had followed the advice given by his captain to the luckless Mr Stewart, the third victim of Cobden's immortal hattrick. At the fifth attempt I contrived to raise the bat and prod the ball gently towards point. After that the feeling of overwhelming pace suddenly vanished; I played a laborious, but enjoyable, innings and made more runs than I ever thought to make again in this world.

So it is very often on fast greens, when we come to them on a sudden. For a few holes we are paralysed, and then the mood of helplessness passes. I remember very well playing on the National Golf Links on Long Island with a very fine American golfer, who later came here with a Walker Cup side. In his native State the greens were very slow, he had never before played at the National. There was a wind blowing and the greens, without being icy keen, were fast. I am not maligning him when I say that in that first round he very seldom took less than three putts, and several times needed four. But he was a good putter, and with another round he had regained his touch and his confidence, and all was well.

So when people say that greens are too fast, let them look to their own putting and see if the fault does not lie there. Let them also be thankful that they live in times when water is laid on, and not when, as in a certain match of Old Tom's at Perth, 'for yards round the hole the grass had gone and a glaze was over all'. Those were the days.

Hard Luck (1952)

'Of course,' said Professor Kennedy, sometime Regius Professor of Greek, 'if I had known that *diamonds* were trumps, I should have played *very* differently.' So at least a Cambridge historian has alleged, adding that the speaker's reproachful tone implied that it was somebody else's fault. It was a fine, bold use of the invaluable 'if', and yet it was paltry compared with that on the grand scale by Romanov, the leader of the Soviet Olympic team at Helsinki. We, in our humility, had believed them to have acquired much merit, but their leader declares that if the footballers, cyclists, swimmers, water-polo players and oarsmen, fencers and horse-men had not all been considerably below their form, and if the referees had been fair, his men would have beaten the Americans. We ourselves have been conducting our own not very profitable *post mortems*, but we cannot, any more than could have Professor Kennedy, live up to this. This is something like an 'if'. We may leave the referee out of the reckoning. The umpire is always wrong, as the ghost of some ancient decision still unforgiven comes back to remind us. L.b.w. forsooth! Why, we played the ball hard and audibly. But that seven sets of players should simultaneously be off their respective games is indeed tragic. As Mr Stiggins once remarked: 'It makes a vessel's heart bleed.' There is no adequate comment. 'Too bad' has somehow an incredulous ring. We can only take refuge in the bald 'Hard Luck!'

We must all sympathise, even though most of us have never

lived up to that imaginary standard which we call our game. In the words of the philosopher William James we have been 'Ever not quite.' Apart, however, from that one general and incomprehensible failure there are so many specific reasons why we have failed. The heartless wretch who moved behind the bowler's arm, the well-meaning idiot who threw a ball into the court during a vital rally, the caddie who had the hiccups, the lark that trilled in the sky – but for these purely fortuitous circumstances the records at the end of the book would be very different. And there is this added poison in our bitter cup, that nobody believes us. This is in some cases our own fault. Honesty is the best policy. If we as much as suspect ourselves of any disease we should declare it before the game starts. It is of no avail when we are as good as beaten. Moreover this open and honourable conduct cuts both ways – we can sometimes do wonderful things when feeling extremely ill, whereby we shall win additional glory. True we shall not gain a character for silent and Spartan endurance, but that was probably lost long ago. The trouble about excuses is that they generally come too late.

A Brave Pursuit (1935)

The final of the British Amateur championship was such a good
and desperately exciting one that all the preceding matches seem
part of a very distant and dim past. A more courageous and relent-
less pursuit than that of Mr Lawson Little by Dr Tweddell has
never been seen on a golf course, and while we are full of praise
for the heroic hunter let us not forget the hunted. The way in
which Mr Little stood up to that long-drawn-out spurt and
ultimately shook it off was magnificent. If anybody had any
doubts – I had not – about his fighting qualities, as apart from his
power of producing 'fireworks', those doubts were resolved by
the grim struggle over the last nine holes.

Most people who are at all interested know by this time the
general run of the match; how Mr Little went off as if he were
going to annihilate his man and was three up at the 4th hole, how
he was then checked and held to his lead of three at lunch; how,
after a slight collapse, he was still three up with ten to go, then
two up and three, dormy two, dormy one, and finally one up. A
match such as this has innumerable 'ifs' and they are essentially
futile things; so I will allow myself no more than two of them.
One belongs to the 5th hole in the first round. Mr Little had a
decidedly short putt there to be four up, and he missed it. At that
moment he was playing as if he meant to 'burn up the course' as
he did at Prestwick the year before. That short putt at once
stopped him a little and gave Dr Tweddell space to breathe. Mr

Little had a 73, which in the wind was very fine golf, but heaven only knows what he might have done if he had not in ever so small a degree been put out of his juggernaut stride. My other 'if' belongs to the second round. Dr Tweddell had won the first two holes and he had the 3rd in the hollow of his hand, but first of all he played a weak pitch and then, with his approach putt, he hit Mr Little's ball. In his turn he let his man off and gave him a welcome breathing space. For a moment it had almost seemed that he had the great man on the run; now for the space of three holes he himself became palpably unsettled. I am not saying for a moment that if Dr Tweddell had won the 3rd hole he would have won the match; that would be absurd. All one can say is that his not winning it seemed at the moment almost tragically important.

That Mr Little was the right man to win and the best golfer in the field no unprejudiced observer could doubt. There is a power and a quality about his game that belonged to nobody else in the same degree. His driving was on the whole as straight as it was long, his long iron shots through and against the wind, and his power of making the ball stop from a short pitch as if it were tethered by a string, were most impressive; his putting was weak now and then, but he was always likely to hole a putt when it was badly needed. Yet Dr Tweddell stood up against a foe thus armed at all points. He did not drive so far, but he constantly drove nearly as far, and only now and again was outdriven by a really important number of yards; he had often to take wood where his opponent only wanted iron, but he was not outplayed in the shots up to the pin; he putted splendidly. The one respect in which he seemed definitely to lose ground was in the short chips from off the green; here Mr Little was always gaining, and yet he cannot have gained much, for what is one hole in thirty-six? I think the fact is that Dr Tweddell has rather a laboured and complex style, and seems to be making the game rather difficult for himself. The spectator, in observing this, does not fully realise what a very fine hitter of the ball, as apart from being a palpably fine fighter, he is.

He is not as good a player as Mr Little, but he did not hang on to him by holing vast putts or laying surprise shots dead; he hung on by playing shot for shot with him. In the course of the week at St Annes I grew rather tired of hearing it said about Mr Little: 'He's not so good as Bobby Jones'. I entirely agree with the remark. Of course he is not. But he is very good indeed, and the mere fact that people think it worth while to make the comparison is as high a compliment as need be. There are not many golfers as to whom it is worth saying, just as there are not many batsmen as to whom anyone would trouble to say: 'He's not as good as W.G.'. Mr Little makes more bad shots than the very greatest golfers have done; yet he does not make many, and I think that his appearance of tremendous physical strength is apt to deceive people. They think of him half unconsciously as a rough-hewn player, but in fact he is a wonderfully accomplished player of iron shots and has a touch of utmost delicacy round the greens.

A Holiday Illusion (1935)

The time of autumn golf has come, and it would be the pleasantest
of the whole year if we could forget that winter golf was hard on
its heels. The touch of wet on the grass, the freshness of the air, if
they did not tell us that summer was over, would promise
delicious rounds. It is the only defect of these October days that
we have to snatch them; we must gather our mushrooms while
we may.

Yet, considered from another aspect autumn is, perhaps, the
most cheerful season of the year. The golfer has come back from
his holiday, and it is then that he dreams the wildest dreams. The
holiday itself is seldom a season for hope, because there is no time
for hoping. It is true that the golfer on his holiday tries this and
that, and often believes that he has got it at last, but disenchant-
ment follows so quickly and so regularly on attainment that it
loses much of its bitterness. He has scarcely had time to pin his
faith to his elbow, before he has discovered the emptiness of all
elbows and turned to his foot. Life is a long series of little dis-
appointments, rather than a single great and tragic one.

When a man comes back to work on the other hand he has
time for reflection; he has been wandering in a crowded mist of
styles; now the mist clears and he sees exactly what he was doing
wrong all the while. He can even remember the round in the
middle of the holiday when he was on the very verge of the great
discovery, only to be led away in another direction by some

perverse will-o'-the-wisp. Yes, that was undoubtedly it, there was a feeling about that particular shot. It was stupid of him not to recognise a thing so obvious at the time, but better late than never. Therefore, the days that elapse between the return home and the first Saturday round are filled with hope, and, given a week, with no chance of sobering disillusion, hope can grow insanely high.

Again the golfer finds it at first pleasant enough to get back to his own course and meet his own partners and opponents. Their characteristic waggles had possibly grown a little tiresome after eleven solid months, but now after an interval he is glad to see them again and to play the old familiar holes. That is an entirely sane and rational pleasure, but here also insanity lurks waiting for its prey. As a rule, the home course is something shorter and easier than the seaside one where the holiday was spent; it is not afflicted by those winds which are, as Mr Guppy would say, 'enough to badger a man blue'. Consequently for the first round or two, golf may seem a comparatively simple game; the gentle suburban breeze does not sweep the ball a hundred yards off the line; if that ball is blown into trouble it can be got out again and is not battered in vain against the remorseless walls of Strath or the Hill bunker. The poor fool actually comes to believe that he has improved and that his holiday resembled a visit to one of those spas which undeniably make a man feel like a limp rag at the time, but are alleged to make him feel like a young Greek god when he gets home again.

This autumnal hopefulness is, in reality, only that which buoys up many golfers from Sunday night to Saturday morning all through the year, but, owing to its slightly exaggerated form, it may endure throughout October with no more than the ordinary ups and downs. With November comes a crash; the golfer finds that he is getting shorter and shorter. If he would accept the fact, which is patent in the case of his friends, that the ground accounts for it, he might be tolerably happy; but the experience of many Novembers has not convinced him, and he goes out practising in the secret dusk in search of that vanished length. There is a particular part of a particular London course that is haunted for me by the friendly ghost of an old gentleman, who was puzzled by this autumnal mystery every year till he was over eighty, and never solved it at last. Let us hope that on Elysian courses there is neither deceitful run nor disillusioning mud.

With regard to this painful subject of mud, I met the other day the sternest and most conscientious of all parents. His home is in a county of clay, so that except on his yearly visit to the greatest of seaside courses he scarcely hits a ball. Not only that but he will not allow his small boys to do so, lest their swings should be corrupted by delving in the mud. I can testify that they swing like dashing young angels, and I look forward to tottering round on a shooting-stick to watch them in future championships; I wonder if a little mud would really hurt them. I recall such good fun in such squelchy fields in my own boyhood that I feel a little sorry for them. I wish they might be allowed just once, on Christmas afternoon, let us say, when they are full of plum pudding. If they solemnly promised to play winter rules and tee the ball they surely could not come to much harm. There is something worse than muddy golf, and that is no golf at all.

Crowd and Urgency
(1945)

We cannot have a great occasion without a crowd. To see and hear in comfort is a desire that grows upon us with age and laziness, but comfort and excitement, though they may live together, can never be true friends. The perfection of poignancy can only be enjoyed by the uncomfortable, and the longing to wave the hat in the air in an ecstasy of triumph is never so keenly felt as when the arms are firmly pinned to the side by the pressure of our next-door neighbours. We may and very likely do hate those neighbours, but they contribute to our excitement for all that, and we feel their thrills not only physically but mentally. The blocked road, the railway carriage with ten people standing in it, the fighting a way to our seats – these are all exquisitely uncomfortable but they add an exquisite flavour to our sensations. Once we grow frightened of them, as I admit I have done, the game is up.

Of the sights enjoyed in youth it is the excitement of the crowd that survives when the spectacle itself has almost wholly vanished from the memory. In 1887 I was taken to see Queen Victoria's Jubilee procession. Save for a general feeling of the unspeakable glory of the Life Guards all has gone. Even the tiny bowing figure in the carriage, the very heart and centre of all that magnificence, has grown very dim. But what remains distinctly is the staying the night before in Kensington, the thrill of early breakfast, the driving as far as the four-wheeler was allowed, and then the walking through yellow sanded streets already lined with people, till the appointed eyrie was reached. That was the crowded hour, there was the glorious life.

I am writing these words soon after watching, in the contemptible luxury of a garden on the river, the University Boat Race. If ever there was an example of the value of crowd and urgency it is this festival. It was a fine sunny day, but with a biting east wind. A million people were there to see, and of those all but the tiniest proportion were at least as ignorant as I am of the art of rowing and had no reason, but a purely artificial partisanship, to care who won. They stood in serried ranks for some hours, they saw the boats for little more than a moment, and for most of the race only the possibility that Cambridge might catch a second crab in that poppling water could avert the inevitable end. That does not sound a particularly enthralling entertainment and yet I have no doubt that those million onlookers found it good fun, and it was good fun.

As far as the race itself was concerned it was all too soon over. There came the cry of 'Here they are' from those perched on a roof nearby, and then the flash of the oars after Hammersmith Bridge, the light blue in front and sparkling cheerfully in the sunlight. For a minute or two we saw the boats and the crowd of following steamers; then they were hidden from us by Chiswick Eyot. The great waves of the steamers surged and splashed against our guardian wall, and after that the river returned once more to comparative emptiness and placidity, the spectators began to disperse, and there was nothing for it but to return indoors to a fire and listen on the wireless to Cambridge – it was Cambridge and that was something – drawing comfortably away to victory.

Nevertheless, I repeat it was uncommonly good fun. There was the packing of the sandwich basket, the settling down to the drive, the wondering whether we should be blockaded as we drew near to Hammersmith, the sight of more and more people obviously making for the river, bent on a common enterprise. It was Hazlitt on the Bath coach going to see the fight at Newbury all over again; on a rather mild scale admittedly, but much can be done by a little imagination. Just because it was a great occasion, the hours

159

of waiting assumed an agreeable tenseness and things ordinarily dull took on a new and vivid interest. We called to each other to look at a procession of steamers, much as we should once have exclaimed at a traction engine thundering down the lane; we felt sorry for the swans rocking in their wash. We watched the spectators accumulating ever more thickly on the Surrey shore and wondered maliciously whether the tide would rise high enough to wet their toes. In short we made the very most of a very little.

Supposing – a singularly futile but pleasing speculation – that we were the Emperor in Hans Andersen's story of 'The Emperor's New Clothes'. If we could decree anything we had a mind to, we might be tempted to order the Boat Race to be rowed for our private and imperial benefit. Even as William Rufus laid waste the New Forest for his hunting, the banks and the bridges should be cleared of onlookers; all the houses along the river must keep their blinds down and we should follow the race sitting under a canopy in a solitary launch blazing with gold. It is a thoroughly disgraceful project and would bring its own reward. We should be proved very stupid and unfit for our position, for the entertainment would fall as flat as a pancake and the oarsmen would scarcely trouble to row, except for the fear of having their heads cut off. And so it would be if any of our other selfish day-dreams could come to pass. A test match, played on the best wicket in the world within our own park palings would lapse into a mere exhibition of skill. Perhaps the most thrilling of all moments in any contest is that of the sudden hush that precedes it, but it would be as nothing if it were only the silence of absent thousands. We might as well hope to get the greatest of all orators to make a speech to us in an empty room as to enjoy a match without the barbarous yells of triumph that greet the fall of a wicket. Without the crowd there can be no urgency.

I, whose business it has been to watch golf, have superficially as good a reason to hate the crowd as have most people. At other games it is kept within bounds but the golf crowd is fluid and pours over the field of play. By much shouting and stewarding and roping it is to some extent restrained, but ever and anon it breaks through and runs wildly and tumultuously. It prevents me from seeing what I want to see, and yet, on purely selfish grounds, I would not be without it, for it can be the most dramatic of all the crowds in the world. The great black ring six deep round the putting green, the silence unbroken save by the curlews calling overhead, is a sight infinitely and eternally exciting. In any golfing scene that I remember over the years the crowd plays its part. How often have I seen – how often, alas! have I described? – John Ball starting down the first hole in a great match with a rose in his button hole, with the trampling and the hum of the prayerful Hoylake crowd behind him, held back by the blue-jerseyed fishermen manning the rope. To ancient hero-worshippers of my generation there never was and never can be again so moving a spectacle as that. But others, second only to it, come back. There is Bobby Jones winning the Open championship at St Andrews. His ball lies in the hollow before the home green, called the Valley of Sin. The crowd are halted solid behind him. The moment he has played his shot and scrambled up the bank, the crowd rush up irresistibly behind him and halt again, making a black fringe round the green. He taps in his winning putt and the next moment there is no inch of green to be seen, nothing but a swirling mob, with Bobby in the middle, perched on adoring shoulders and his putter, 'Calamity Jane', held in precarious safety over his head.

Even more tremendous, in point of sheer numbers, is the scene of our lone victory in the Walker Cup, when all but one match is finished, and the individual crowds that have been watching the others come streaming over the burn, with divisions melting into corps, and corps into one great army, converging on the cockpit of the home green. Better a thousand times to have been crushed and buffeted, and to have seen little but 'the 'oofs of the 'orses' than to have missed so splendidly terrifying a spectacle. To-day at St Andrews we who watch are herded to the side-lines among the whins. It has to be for the sake of the players and we ourselves see far more than we used to do, if at longer range, but something of the old drama has departed.

A Warrior Taking His Rest (1930)

'There's always one thing to look forward to – the Sunday morning round at Old Eastlake with nothing to worry about when championships are done.' Three years ago Mr Bobby Jones wrote those words, the last words in *Down the Fairway* and now, sooner perhaps than he then expected, the dimly seen future has become the present and his championships are done.

The announcement that he meant to retire came as something of a bombshell. We should not perhaps have been much surprised if he had announced it after winning the last of his four championships at Merion, but he made no sign and almost lulled us into a sense of security. Only the day before it happened I was lunching with two good golfers and we were discussing whether or not he would play in championships again, little anticipating that we were on the point of having our question answered. We did not all agree. One member of the party thought that he could, and would, play occasionally in championships and take things, by comparison, easily. I held that to do that was not consistent with his temperament and that he had better take the plunge now at the very climax of his career. It is dreadfully sad to think that we shall not watch him winning our championship again but for myself I am as nearly as I can be glad that he has made this decision.

How much that decision has been affected by his undertaking to make an 'educational' film it is hard to say. The whole question of such a film is a difficult one. Lesser players have written books and articles professing to teach people how to play, and no-one has declared them not to be amateurs. Here is something that might, perhaps, be said not to be different in kind but only in degree. As Bobby says in his statement, 'A lot might be said on either side', but, whatever the exact law may be, he has shown the right feeling in being conscious that many people would hold his action, an entirely honourable one in itself, contrary to the spirit of amateurism. By deciding to retire from championships before entering on this new work he has spared his friends the discomfort of making a difficult and possibly painful decision and, if he has any enemies, he has deprived them of a chance of showing their malice. As far as this point is concerned he has behaved not only discreetly, but like, what he has always been, a good golfer.

To my mind he has been equally wise in deciding that he has borne the heavy strain long enough, and that he wants to play golf for 'recreation and enjoyment'. That it has been a desperately heavy strain no-one who knows him can doubt; nor would it become lighter just because he has won so many times that no defeat could affect his position. Players of a different nature might find it possible to play at half pressure. I do not think Bobby could do that in a championship. As long as he is playing for it he must strain every nerve to win. From the fiery young prodigy, who was rebuked by the newspapers for sometimes throwing his clubs about, he has turned himself into a model of icily imperturbable deportment, but he has not found the game less hard work for that. 'I read a line somewhere,' he says, 'or a title, "The Cage of Championships". *It is*, something like that, something like a cage. First you are expected to get into it, and then you are expected to stay there. But of course nobody can stay there. Out you go – and then you are trying your hardest to get back in again. Rather silly, isn't it, when golf – just golf – is so much fun?' In those words are summed up many of his reasons for retiring, and there is much sound sense in them. They may be taken, I suppose, also to represent the views of Miss Joyce Wethered. It is rather an illuminating fact that we now have the two greatest golfers in the world, Miss Wethered and Mr Jones, both tired of battles and conquests at the age of twenty-nine and longing to play golf for fun.

It seems a long time now since Bobby first came here. It is, in fact, nine years since he played in the Amateur championship at Hoylake. He was then only nineteen, but already had been a celebrity for five years. I remember very well when I was in Macedonia, in 1916, reading of the infant phenomenon who had just appeared at Merion, and thinking that this was one of the golfers I wanted to watch if the confounded war ever ended. In 1919 he had been runner-up in the American Amateur championship, and already his admirers were becoming most bitterly disappointed that at his then mature age he had not yet managed to be champion outright. In that Hoylake championship, on the hardest, keenest ground I think I ever saw, his golf was of an extraordinarily mixed kind. He began by playing quite well against the late Mr Manford, and then relapsed into an absurd game – for him – against Mr Hamlet of Wrexham, who went round in about 88, took Bobby to the home hole, and might very well have beaten him if he could have holed a shortish putt on the Royal green. Next he murdered Mr Harris, against whom he always seemed to be brilliantly unkind, and then Mr Allan Graham, as he describes it himself, 'fairly beat him to death with a queer brass putter'. After that he went to St Andrews for the Open championship and, after a disastrous encounter with the 11th hole, drove his ball into the sea, a very natural proceeding, for which he was unnecessarily apologetic.

As far as the results were concerned, that was rather a disappointing visit for him, but everybody who then saw him realised that sooner or later he must win, not merely something, but everything. It is odd to recall now what is, I am sure, a fact, that the comparatively weak spot in his game was then his putting. Of late years it has been the wonderfully consistent goodness of his putting that, more than anything else, has accounted for his victories; other champions have had their on days and off days on the green, but he always putts at least as well as any other man in the field. In 1921, whereas nearly all the other members of the American team struck the ball in that smooth, precise, mechanical way which is so characteristic, Bobby had something more of the 'caddy-boy' method, rather lacking in smoothness and not holding out promise of steadiness. He changed all that soon afterwards, and now his putting is surely the most perfect example of rhythm that ever was seen; but it is worth recording as a historic fact that we have seen Bobby Jones when he was not a great putter, and hardly even a good one.

I am not going to set out the record of his later visits. Everybody knows that St Annes, Hoylake and St Andrews – twice over – are the battle honours inscribed on his crowded flag. So far as it was possible for his popularity here to increase, it has increased with each of his visits, and it is pleasant to remember that he is not only the most distinguished of our golfing visitors, but an ordinary member of one of our golf clubs, the Royal and Ancient. That is a comforting thought, because we may hope that he will some day come back to play – owing an incredible number of strokes to scratch – in the Jubilee Vase, or to try to beat, in the Autumn Medal, his championship record of 68. Meanwhile we must wait to see him on his famous film. If it does not improve our golf – a thing past hoping for in some cases – it will at least give us a sight of a cherished friend.

Failure of Nerve (1912)

There is probably no game which affords a greater scope than golf for all possible forms of nervousness, not only for sheer terror but for every conceivable foolish fancy which can impair the properly concentrated frame of mind. It is so horribly deliberate and long drawn out that it is impossible to make the mind a blank; and it may be safely laid down that there is not a golfer in the world who has not at times felt a paralysing sensation creeping over him.

The ordinary player, with ordinarily bad nerves, can master them far more successfully on one day than on another, and that without knowing the reason why. A comparatively short run of victories even over quite insignificant opponents is apt to breed an astonishing and most serviceable confidence. The victor may not have played more than passably well; he may not be under any particular delusion as to the merit of his performance, but still he attains that happy frame of mind in which he believes that things will come right and not wrong in the end, and that he will 'muddle through' somehow. It has been said before that the man is 'on his game' who does not mind making a bad shot, and this enviable state is generally produced by a run of good luck. If, on the other hand, his run has been one of bad luck, he goes to meet trouble something more than half way, and hails the first bad shot as the beginning of the end – the end both of his match and also of the particular new system of driving, pitching, or putting which with faint and trembling hope he has just invented.

One of the most distressing features of the complaint is that the victim never knows when and where it will seize him in its grip. He may begin his match by feeling, to his intense surprise, mildly bored with the proceedings; that is generally bad, since this lethargy may never wear off and he may be beaten through a sheer inability to try. Again, he may start with a magnificent and stoical calm, and all may go well for a while. Then, just when he is rejoicing in this Heaven-sent mood, he may make one mistake, and with scarcely any warning find himself prostrated by a sudden wave of nervousness. This is perhaps the worst of all things that can befall him, since it is doubly difficult to recover from the unexpected. To find himself trembling like a leaf upon the first tee, although in itself unpleasant, does not always presage disaster; for thus he sometimes suffers the worst agonies before the real struggle begins; and if things go passably well for a hole or two, he gets into his stride and maintains it to the end.

The curious tricks that nerves can play upon their owners are particularly well illustrated by matches that go to the 19th hole. Take by way of example two of the matches in the English Ladies' championship, played not long since at Prince's, Sandwich. Two ladies were dormy six and dormy five up respectively upon their opponents; in each case the leader lost all the remaining holes and the match was halved; then, on proceeding to the 19th (or, as in one case, to the 21st) hole, the player who had lost her long lead in so demoralising a fashion pulled herself together and won after all. Nor is this apparently singular occurrence to be seen solely in ladies' championships, for it was only in the summer of 1911 in the American championship that Mr Hilton, after having stood some five or six holes up on Mr Herreshoff, lost every single hole of his lead and won at the 37th hole. Yet another example may be given from Mr Hilton's career. When he beat Mr Low in the final match of the Amateur championship at St Andrews in 1901 he stood five up with thirteen to play, was pulled back to all square and two to play, and then, by playing two holes as well as they could humanly be played, won by a single hole. In fact the occurrence is so comparatively common that, however unaccountable, it must be reckoned among the things that may be expected to happen.

Unaccountable at first sight it most certainly is. The player who lets a long lead slip away from him is always in a more or less nervous, miserable and peevish condition; he who has snatched a match apparently lost out of the fire is, on the other hand, confident and triumphant. It would seem that the nerve-racking experience of a 19th hole should only accentuate the difference between these two opposite frames of mind. Yet as a fact the tide seems as often as not to turn with these extra holes. So long as he has any lead still to dissipate the leader plays in a faint-hearted manner, as if lamenting over the irrevocable past instead of devoting himself to the present. When every hole is squandered and his back is against the wall, a sort of fierce composure seems to settle down upon him; he really concentrates his mind and really fights. But the success of this last desperate rally should not perhaps be wholly attributed to him that makes it, because the adversary has also undergone a revulsion of feeling. When he was five or six holes down he thought of avoiding, not defeat, but disgrace; the possibility of victory itself probably did not definitely obtrude itself until very nearly the end of the round. When, however, he has wiped out the whole of that crushing deficit and faces the tee once more an unburdened man, the almost miraculous nature of his escape thrusts itself upon him; he reflects that to lose now, after all he has gone through, would be insupportably bitter; he falters for an instant, and in that one instant is undone. The picturesque role of the heroic and indomitable pursuer is in some ways more easy to support, so long as there seems no real chance of the pursuit being crowned with success.

James Braid: A Man of Character (1952)

The future golfing historian will doubtless perceive that during
the lifetime of James Braid and his distinguished contemporaries
the position of the golf professional became an altogether different one, alike in reward and in social status. It is not so certain
whether he will appreciate how much that difference was due to
their fine example in character and conduct. Unquestionably
their chance came with the immense spread of the game in their
time but it was by the way they took that chance that they showed
themselves the men they were. In their boyhood's days there were
very few greens that needed or could afford a professional and so,
unless he was one of the few lucky and resolute ones, he never rose
far above the status of the caddie from which he had originally
emerged, and when hard times or old age overtook him he ended
as he had begun. If he was inclined to drink too much, as he often
was, he was not greatly to be blamed, for his life produced
naturally many idle hours and drink was one obvious way in
which to pass them.

At the time when James and his contemporaries were emerging
from boyhood the professional's opportunities were improving.
In the later 'eighties when he was seventeen or eighteen the game
was spreading like wildfire over England and the demand for
someone who should combine the greenkeeper, the club-maker
and the teacher was in consequence rapidly increasing. But even
so it did not till a few years later offer a very inviting prospect and
it is easy to understand how James's parents thought that a safe

steady-going job as a joiner was a wiser investment than a plunge into the wild unknown England, where their lovable but reprehensible relation, Douglas Rolland, had taken sanctuary from the stern edicts of his native land.

By the time James had decided to take the plunge the prospects in England were perceptibly brighter, and not only there, for the game was likewise booming in Scotland. There was now a real chance for a steady man to make a decent living and, if he were an outstanding player, something more than that. But the margin of profit was still small and the player's rewards inconsiderable. To win a prize of £10 on the way to the Open championship brought with it the comfortable assurance that at least the expenses of the visit were provided for. To be a good player was by no means enough; the professional must be ready to turn his hand to anything: mending a club one minute; rolling the green or if need be digging a new bunker the next; ruling as caddie master over a herd of boys. It was a hard and busy life and beyond all these multifarious duties the club professional must be ever ready to make himself pleasant to all sorts and conditions of members, most of them ready no doubt to be pleasant themselves, but a few of them exacting and unreasonable to an infuriating degree. All these difficult things James and his great contemporaries achieved in a truly remarkable degree; always dignified and always respectful; steadily raising the whole status of their profession as they raised themselves; models of good and natural manners on and off the course. They set a wonderful example and the good they did will live long after them.

Apart from this universal esteem and respect felt for himself and his colleagues, James had a truly remarkable power of inspiring affection. This became more and more noteworthy in his later years, for we have as a nation a deep and genuine feeling for a grand old man in any walk of life and not least a grand old game-player. But throughout his career he had had the gift of making people fond of him. Up to a point it is not difficult for a prominent player of games to inspire personal liking, and it is perhaps easier for golfers than for the heroes of other games, since in the nature of their game they are surrounded and hemmed in by potential admirers, longing to repeat a single word overheard or, still better, to extract one addressed to themselves. To suffer them gladly is one of the tasks to which the Champion must school himself, and he must also learn, if he can, to make some pretence of remembering the man who said 'Well played' at the 10th hole on a course never visited before or since some dozen years ago. A golfer who, like the members of the Triumvirate, [Braid, Taylor and Vardon] plays in the course of years at numberless different places must inevitably be in the position of having met in a flash of lightning thousands of people of whom he has not the faintest recollection. But they remember him vividly, often crediting themselves with a familiarity with the great man which is wholly illusory, and retailing the mildest of small stories of what he said or did. Even as the Duke of Wellington was 'much exposed to authors' so James was much exposed to spectators of this kind and nobody was better qualified to deal with them. His invincible tranquillity made him endure their untimely interruptions and his memory was such that he sometimes did, contrary to all the laws of probability, really remember them.

These qualities naturally made for a general liking, but such a popularity as almost any champion can command, is very different from the real, deep affection that not only his friends but thousands who had barely exchanged a word with him felt for James. His was not merely that negative popularity such as is sometimes gained by silent and reserved men. James was beyond all doubt reserved, almost to a point of being secretive; he did not like garrulous people; he said very little and could hardly ever be said to let himself go. He certainly never seemed to go out of his way to seek affection, and if he felt it for others, as I am convinced he did, I doubt if he ever expressed it in words. He might have felt it altogether too gushing and barely decent to do so; yet it was an essentially positive affection that innumerable people felt for him and one that grew ever warmer with the years.

James was a monument of two invaluable qualities, common sense and discretion. It is impossible to think of his doing or saying a foolish thing and though he heard much he revealed nothing. If, as has been said, 'philosophy is nothing but discretion', then James was well worthy to be called a philosopher. Moreover he had more than common sense, he had wisdom. I think that on any problem of which he was by experience competent to judge he would have given as sound advice as it was possible to obtain. If he did not feel competent, nothing would have induced him to say a word. 'His virtues walked their narrow round' but within that round there could not have been a more trustworthy counsellor, nor one who would think out a question more thoroughly before giving an opinion on it.

It may be said perhaps that the natural bent of his mind was cautious and conservative. He would look more than once before he leaped, and his first inclination was to say, 'I would not do it'. But there was about him this comforting and compensating quality that if his advice was in favour of doing it, whatever it was, it was pretty sure to be the right and wise thing to do. The very last words he spoke at a meeting of the Professional Golfers' Association almost immediately before going into the nursing home for his operation, were extremely characteristic of his restraining wisdom, 'Take care you don't cut your own throats'.

He had, as everybody must have, his likes and dislikes among people, but it would have taken an extraordinarily keen observer to guess at them from his calm, dignified, unchanging good manners. As he was a generous man in his everyday life, so he was a generous opponent at golf, and the same high praise must be given to his illustrious adversaries. They were constantly trying to beat one another and for several years the highest honours were very nearly confined to their small group. Each of them wanted with his whole soul to win, for no one can attain to such a position as was theirs without a fierce desire for victory; but they remained magnanimously equal to either fortune. It is not in human nature never to feel some grievance against the Fates in defeat and some envy of the victor, but whatever they felt they gave no sign of their emotions and remained models of good losing as of good winning.

In the evening Braid would often go across the road from his house to the social club in Walton, of which he was an original member. Here he would occasionally play darts but his more regular game was billiards. A great player he was not but he drove the balls about the table with much of that 'divine fury' which Horace Hutchinson had attributed to him in golf so many years before, sometimes with results very disconcerting to the opposition.

The club never taught him to smoke. He had given it a very brief trial in his youth and decided firmly against it. His life at home remained in many ways as it always had been. Though he made so many journeys he would never have a car, but stuck to a train, not on economic grounds but because he was always prone to car sickness. He also refused to have a telephone and that was probably an example of his natural shrewdness; he knew that he would be given too little peace if he had it.

I suppose the thought of retiring must now and then inevitably have occurred to him but only as an ultimate and distant possibility. When the reporters asked him on his eightieth birthday whether he meant to retire he entirely and, I am convinced, genuinely denied it. Why should he retire? He loved his work and the play that was part of it. Whenever there was a competition at Walton Heath he was there to start the players and if need be to help manage the crowd. When the Daily Mail tournament was played there during the last summer of his life I saw him positively run, not very far and not very fast, but still run to shoo away an intrusive onlooker. He would have been lost without his life's work and it ought perhaps to be a cause for thankfulness that he never had to endure life without it.

American Contrasts (1922)

I was watching at Brookline the final of the American championship between Mr Jesse Sweetser and Mr Chick Evans. The next
golf that I saw, some eleven days later, was in the final of the
Girls' championship at Stoke Poges between Miss Muriel Wicken-
den and Miss Barbara Griffiths. The contrast was a vivid one, and
has made me try to set down some of the differences between golf
in the two countries.

Both these young ladies have the makings of fine golfers and
can play a great deal better then they did in that final. If they
played some very bad strokes, they also played some good and
gallant ones, strokes that would have roused an American crowd
to frenzied applause; but – here was the first contrast – the gallery
at Stoke remained entirely placid. Only once was there a mild
demonstration, when one of the players after a severe struggle
just extracted herself from a deep bunker. On that occasion a
sardonic spectator remarked, 'I wonder which they are clapping,
the lady or the bunker, because it seems to me the bunker had the
best of it.'

The habit of clapping at golf matches has greatly increased in
this country during the last few years but we still lag far behind in
that respect, and I confess to hoping that we may continue to do
so. Another contrast is that, apart from the state of the match,
whether his own or somebody else's, the American golfer takes a
tremendous interest in the score. We have been brought up to

think this is in a match rather tiresome and, personally, I am too old to change my views. The fact that in a four-ball match in America everybody is inclined to hole out, whether or not his score has any effect on the match, makes for a slow progress round the course. Nevertheless, I believe that this habit, though it might not suit us, improves the average American golfer's play. By reason of it he never gets slack, he is always trying, so that trying becomes a second nature; he is continually interested and amused and ambitious and has a genuine standard by which to judge his improvement or deterioration.

These two contrasts are matters of temperament. Now I come to one of another sort which is very striking. I never fully realised till I was in America this time what a difference wind makes in the game. The vast majority of American golfers play upon sheltered inland courses. They have very little wind, and as to playing in a real seaside gale, many a good sound player there does not begin to imagine it. In addition to this, the greens are not cut very short for fear of the burning sun, and they are regularly watered. Consequently the play up to the hole appears to British eyes a little monotonous and in a sense artificial. Nearly all the greens are closely bunkered, and in any case the grassy turf does not lend itself to the running shot, so that the approach is nearly always a high pitching stroke, of varying lengths of course, right up to the holeside.

There is a certain sameness about this stroke and I hasten to add, there is, to their opponents, an admirable and alarming sameness about the way in which the Americans play it. They are quite wonderfully straight and accurate. Most of them use to some extent the ribbed clubs, which here are barred and now and again they gain by doing so. I shall never forget one shot played by my opponent in the International match – a pitch, if anything downwind, on to a tiny little plateau, which made the ball stop literally within two feet. Generally speaking, however, with the greens slow and soft, a high shot with an ordinary club will stop the ball quite quickly enough. This high shot many good American golfers play in a manner that we have always been taught to avoid. With much lofted clubs, in the nature of mashie-niblicks, they take practically a full swing, such as they would with wooden clubs and follow it through. And, whether or not this is contrary to what all the wise men have told us, they are extraordinarily straight, and time and again the ball comes plump down close to the hole and leaves the player a putt for a birdie. There is Mr Knepper, for instance, who beat Mr Tolley after one of the most dramatic and blood-curdling matches that was ever seen. He seems to be playing just one short all the time with his iron club, till he comes to a really short chip. It is in the nature of a full swinging shot and I have seen very few players more diabolically accurate, more unswervingly straight. If there was a high wind this shot would not do, and because Mr Knepper is a very good player he would doubtless soon cultivate some other. As it is, he has never been forced to do so and so sticks to the one shot which he has thoroughly mastered and has paid him so well.

A Form of Obloquy (1945)

Whether it is some inheritance of primeval savagery from remot-
est ancestors or whether it is no more than a natural healthy
instinct, let the psychologists determine; I do not know. All I say
is that for the normal human being the moment of keenest,
sensuous pleasure any game has to offer is that of hitting as hard as
heaven and his bodily powers will allow him. As he grows older
and feebler he must taste it vicariously in watching the hitting of
others, yet that thrill of quivering joy is still essentially the same.

It is the vehemence of the blow rather than the consequences
that produces the ecstasy. I never received a more vivid impression
of hard hitting at its exciting best than in watching the champions
of badminton attack so murderously the poor little shuttlecock
that is only capable of fluttering a few yards. In the making up to
strike, as it were the drawing back for a spring, in the throwing of
every ounce of muscle into the stroke at exactly the right instant,
in the sense of zest and power, here was as much to enjoy and
admire as in the longest drive at golf or a hit into the highest point
of the pavilion at Lord's.

Within a few days of that almost terrifying experience I watched
by happy chance the great men of table tennis, and came away
equally stunned and overpowered. Nobody who has not seen the
modern game – and I have seen it but once – can realise how
different it is from that which he played himself in ancient days,
perhaps on no more formal or statutory battlefield than the dining-

room table. Gone are those interminable bouts of neat little back-handed half-volleys in which he used complacently to indulge, deeming himself something of a triton among the domestic minnows. The rallies can still be long, since there are spells of comparatively defensive play, and the power of retrieving the apparently impossible is beyond belief; but that which primarily strikes an awe and terror upon the sight is the tremendous driving.

Those two brief experiences convinced me that it is the hardness that counts and not the distance that results from the hit. Consider for an instant the question of the golf ball. Whenever it is proposed to keep its flight, and so incidentally the dimension of the course, within reasonable limits, golfers are up in arms, each man fearing that his own drives will be clipped of a few yards of distance. Now and again they can reach a particular landmark at a particular hole. If they could do so no more they fancy their little world would come toppling in ruins about them. Fools that they are! they do not realise that length is relative; the positive pleasure is in the hitting. The distance that the ball travels may vary but that physical satisfaction is constant and unvarying. It would be idle to deny that it is good fun to see the ball go swooping away over hill or valley for enormous distances. We cannot refrain from the same child-like 'Oh' of delight with which we greet a rocket at the fireworks. But if the ball were ever reduced in power we should quickly readjust our standards and be equally swept off our feet by an achievement in point of mere yards more modest.

The greatest drive I ever witnessed – certainly it gave me the greatest thrill – still seems to me one made by a professional on Coldham Common at Cambridge over sixty years ago. I can still see in imagination the ball soaring into the mist which hung about that place of mud and gloom. Yet today the same length would doubtless be attained with a light iron. Einstein's theory of relativity is of course beyond my comprehension, but I have my own theory of relativity in regard to hitting to which I am indissolubly wedded.

Some of us cannot hit as hard as others, but the joy is in hitting as hard as we can. Whatever the game, that is not to be attained unless we do it in the right way, for hard hitting is not, as the envious sometimes allege, only a question of brute strength, though strength is important; it is also and most emphatically one of skill. Much of the pleasure of seeing it is in the pose and rhythm of the hitter. There is a moment of bracing, of tension, and then everything the player possesses pours in a smooth, yet irresistible flow into the ball. 'One of the most beautiful sights that can be imagined,' wrote Nyren of William Beldham, 'and which would have delighted an artist, was to see him make himself up to hit a ball. It was the beau ideal of grace, animation and concentrated energy.' That description might serve for any great player and any kind of ball. The instant of 'making up' is but as a flash; if it be more there is a suggestion of heaviness and effort, but just that instant there must be, for the perfection of the mysterious and heaven-sent gift that we call timing. The more clearly inspired the hitter, the more conspicuous is the appearance of leisure, that he has all the time in the world in which to hit. 'Even in his hard hitting,' wrote Alfred Lyttelton of William Gray, 'there was an ease and grace delightful to watch ... In games he would frequently use old rackets apparently as unfitted for active service as the seats of old cane-bottomed chairs. But in his hand those veterans seemed to renew their youth and drove in a manner that was both astonishing and mortifying to an opponent who, with an incomparably superior tool, produced most inferior results.' There is a fine relish in the words, a picture of genius given only to the very few.

If he be graceful he can scarcely be too murderous for our bloodthirsty taste. I doubt if any game has ever provided a more truly awful spectacle than that of Mr Edward Blackwell driving a golf ball; a big man with a big, heavy club which he wielded as if it were a toy. His swing though extremely rapid was smooth and lovely and, while there was no undue appearance of effort, he was yet so palpably out for blood. He put everything he had into the stroke; as one admirer wrote, he even put his eyebrows into it, and they were essentially formidable eyebrows. There was about him

179

the same 'divine fury' which Horace Hutchinson attributed to James Braid, and Braid, tearing a ball away from a hanging lie, going down to fetch it, as it were, with his knees buckling beneath him, provided a sight comparable in magnificence.

'Elegance, all elegance, fit to play before the King in his parlour.' That was said of Joseph Guy, one of the batsmen, by the way, to whom Prowse awarded a rather grudging meed of praise in his poem on Alfred Mynn. It is a charming picture. But we, the great mass of hearty, ignorant spectators, want something more than that; we want venom. It is noteworthy when we watch cricket how swiftly and greedily the appetite for hits comes in the eating. One boundary may receive little more than a formal acknowledgment, but if the next ball goes the same way our spirits and our tributes rise immeasurably. In the summer of 1947 I watched a day's play in the Test match against the South Africans at Lord's, in which Compton and Edrich were making a big stand, running neck and neck in the matter of runs, with Compton a little ahead. The scoring was of a good pace but always discreet. We were all happy and all liberal with our applause, but in a comparatively restrained manner. Then there came on an unfortunate slow bowler and Edrich suddenly cut loose and hit his first four balls for four of the most exhilarating boundaries. The first was clapped, the second cheered, and the third and fourth produced a crescendo of shouts and crows and delighted laughter. That cheerful hitting had gone to our heads like wine.

In all four of the strokes the ball had clung virtuously to the ground. We should, I fancy, have crowed still more loudly if in one of them it had soared into the air. It is perhaps a confession of weakness but the most inebriating of all hits is undeniably one that climbs the sky, and the higher the better. A series of perfect shots along the floor leave on the memory, when the day is over, only a blurred and general vision of magnificence, but one outrageous six may remain for ever. It is doubtless very wrong, but then, contrary to all propriety, we do remember the wrong things.

There can be no stroke in any game so suggestive of pure savagery as the whole-hearted smash at tennis executed by a master hand. It seems almost too brutal

> 'It's like hitting of a gal,
> It's a lubberly thing for to do.'

But it must be productive of the most exquisite sensations, over which to lick the chops of memory. How sad that, save on the rarest occasions, they are out of the reach of the common man. When I used sometimes to play lawn tennis, to give my form of it that courtesy title, I found that by a niggling, sneaking game of ineffable meanness I could sometimes beat those of more soaring ambitions, because their strokes soared far out of court. I had a profound contempt for my own methods, but I had also a shameful and irrepressible desire to win, and in the humble circles in which I moved those methods were not wholly un-profitable.

It seems to me that for those who have not learned and prob-ably never will learn to hit the ball properly, that is for the great mass of mankind, there is much to be said for a game played in a court wholly surrounded by walls. To say so much is not to insult one of the noblest of all games, rackets. Rackets has a splendour that explains itself to the least educated eye. The glory of hitting reaches the highest possible point, and the ball travels almost at the speed of thought. In thinking over the gratification derived from all kinds of great hitters, I incline to put first that of the only occasion on which I watched Mr J. C. F. Simpson in a racket court. Neither for the world would I affront squash, truly exciting when played by the best, while for the worst it is, to quote Peter Latham's scornful aphorism, 'banging about in a box'; and that in a most cheering form, for at least they do bang. That is why I am upholding for the humble and meek those surrounding walls. They will not help the weakling to win, for his most violent blows will only present his enemy with an easy chance off the back wall, but they will help him to enjoy himself. He will now and again give the ball one blow with all his might and main;

most likely to no purpose, but it will afford him a sensation of virility. In that ecstatic moment at least he will have lived.

Hard hitting has some of the great qualities of obloquy. It is like telling a man for once in a while what we really think of him. It may be that from Christian or even prudential motives we had better have refrained. Our vocabulary may have been miserably inadequate but we have done our best. We have screwed ourselves up to the effort which imparts a glow to the still trembling frame. In that supreme instant we reck little of the consequences. So it is with our more passive enemy the ball. We have let it have it for all we are worth, we have got under the tail of that one. Let it vanish into the thickest whins or the depths of the sea! *Ruat coelum*! We have hit it hard.

An Attack of Socketing (1935)

People who talk too much about their ailments are justly deemed to be bores. Yet there are one or two complaints the mention of which will, as a rule, produce a general and spirited conversation. If, for instance, one has anything the matter with one's knee or back and says so in company, one is at once overwhelmed by advice as diverse as it is sympathetic, since every one of the auditors knows the one man in the world who can cure knees and backs as if by magic. Similarly in the case of golfing ailments, almost every golfer has at some time or another had an attack of the fearful disease called 'socketing', and will take his part in the talk if the latest victim starts the subject. Some, indeed, refrain not so much because they think the topic tiresome as because they think it too dreadful. Having been stricken and cured, they wish to forget all about the attack lest the mere thought of it should bring a recurrence. Such people had better skip the rest of this article, because I propose to describe a short, or at least I hope short, and severe attack of socketing which lately befell a golfer whose game I know better than I do anyone else's in the world.

This golfer, who has played the game now for a depressingly long time, has never been seriously troubled by socketing. He once had a mild visitation, in consequence of which he bought a crook-necked mashie and mashie-niblick supposed to make impossible the hitting of a non-existent socket. He grew so fond of them that he has played with them ever since – that is, for twelve or thirteen years – and, in cases of extreme mental anguish, has even gone so far as to putt with the mashie. Just once, for the space of a shot or two, he discovered that it was possible to socket with the socketless club, but he has been practically immune from the disease. Suddenly, like a thunderbolt out of a blue sky, it descended on him.

I believe that pride nearly always comes before a fall in such cases, and my golfer was playing, or thought he was playing, rather well with that crook-necked mashie. He was hitting the ball with plenty of 'nip' and confidence: he was in a complacent state of mind and inclined to take liberties. One day he went out into the field next door to his house to play a few shots for air and exercise. He had on a good many clothes, and his braces felt rather tight, but what did that matter? He knew he could hit the ball, and for a few minutes he did hit it so accurately that he was lost in admiration of the perfect grouping of the balls in the smallest possible space at just the point he was aiming at. Then without the least warning a ball sped skimming the grass in the direction of cover-point. He laughed – a little uneasily and artificially – and addressed himself to another ball. That one went nearer point than cover-point, and of the next dozen balls nine or ten did exactly the same thing.

Anybody who has ever suffered will know what were his sensations. He felt as if Heaven's worst curse had suddenly fallen on him and he had gone mad. In other respects he appeared to himself to be normal; the scenery had not changed; the field and the dripping trees and the depressed cows in one corner looked just as they had ten minutes before. The thing in his hand was almost certainly a mashie (warranted not to socket); the thing on the grass was a ball which he was addressing in what he believed to be his usual way; he was looking at it very hard and swinging very slow; and yet – there went another one, further to the right than ever. The hour of lunch was approaching. When he went in to eat it, his family would probably discover that he was raving mad and would send for the doctor; he would be removed to an asylum. Meanwhile (O heavens! look at that one!) he must and would hit one ball not on the socket before the gong summoned him to his doom. In the nick of time a notion came into his disordered brain, and one, two, three balls were hit straight; his deportment at lunch was not detected as being insane; perhaps he was not mad, after all.

He rushed out again afterwards, having first taken off some of those superfluous garments, and, except for one horror, there were no more socketings; but he played each shot with a most elaborate carefulness, even as a drunken man speaks when he is uncertain of his powers of articulation. Whether he is really cured it is too early to say, and in any case it is doubtful whether he will ever be the same man again. The shock of that sudden visitation is not easily forgotten, and the undeniably humorous circumstances of his socketing with a socketless club will not mend matters. I am apprehensive about the poor fellow's future.

It is conceivable that others who have suffered may ask how the attack was cured. Well, I am not quite sure. Socketing comes and goes, and I have always observed that golfing doctors are chary of prescribing for it. 'A medical winner,' remarked Sir Walter Simpson, 'unable to hit with any part except the socket of his iron is no uncommon phenomenon.' But he laid down no precise treatment. As far as I could discover in my poor friend's case, both his previous complacency and his superfluous clothing had something to do with it. Both because he was self-satisfied and because he had too many clothes on for proper swinging, he tried to hit the ball with too much wrist and too little of anything else. Also, I fancied that his right elbow was not clinging to his side as it ought, but flying out from the body on the way down. At any rate, it was by trying to be very stiff and to keep that elbow under control that he checked the pestilence; but, for all I know, both the cause of the attack and the manner of its arrest were really quite other than those I have described.

I recollect that a good while ago this poor man won a certain tournament. In one of the rounds the enemy had come to such sad grief at the last hole that my friend could not fail to win if he kept topping the ball down the middle of the course. He remarked to an onlooker: 'Thank Heaven, I've got a mashie without a socket', and by trundling the ball in inglorious safety with this weapon he duly won. If he had known then what he has learned now I doubt whether he would ever have reached the green at all. Meanwhile, I do hope that, by describing his torments in such detail, I shall not have put socketing into somebody else's head, especially into the head of somebody who has socketless clubs. That would, I admit, be an impish, not to say a malignant thing to do.

Easing the Strain (1921)

The habit of control is equally valuable whether in match or medal play, but the particular quality of strain to be borne varies with the form of game – or torture – in which we are indulging. In medal play it is longer and more continuous, in match play more acute at certain moments. Some people can endure, may actually enjoy, the one, some the other. In match-play, of which we have hitherto been talking, it is the unexpectedness of a shock that often destroys us – a miraculous recovery by the enemy followed by a missed putt of our own – the entire tragedy making a difference of two holes. In a medal it is true that one mistake may be almost fatal, but though we may be frightened of the big bunkers, it is not they that ruin us. Again, though we may give ourselves unpleasant shocks, at least we cannot receive them from anyone else. There is no living adversary for us to endure in imagination with an infallibility that he is far from possessing. In a medal round we simply beat ourselves. Much dripping wears away a stone, and continual fussing and fretting, with never a breathing space such as there may be in a match, wears away the golfer. It is nearly always the putting that does it. If you take a walk on a medal day you will see the most ludicrously bad putting. The approach putts are nearly always short, and as to the holing out you would think that half the players were suffering from some painful disease of the wrist – so stiffly do they poke and prod at the ball with never a free wrist amongst them. Sir Walter Simpson declared that the only way to putt well in a medal round was to putt carelessly. It is a paradox with a great deal of truth in it.

Much of this terror comes from our playing so few scoring rounds. Familiarity breeds, if not contempt of the scoring card, at least some respect for ourselves. It is very good discipline, too, and if the American amateurs are going ahead of us now, I suspect they owe a good deal to the constant succession of thirty-six or eighteen holes of score play with which their tournaments begin. Anybody, and especially any young golfer who is in earnest about improving his game and his temperament, ought, I am sure, to play as many medal rounds as he can. Let him scour the country for open meetings and never disdain the humble monthly medal. He will be called a pot-hunter by his more otiose or timorous friends, but he will get his reward.

I do not know that there are many categorical 'don'ts' for a medal player, but I am sure there is one, namely, don't hang about for some time on the tee before your turn comes. Abe Mitchell's dramatic collapse in the third round of last year's Open championship, when he seemed to have the first prize in his pocket, is now historical. One can never be certain what might or might not have happened, but assuredly Mitchell did himself no good, and perhaps a great deal of harm, by being down at the course far earlier than he need have been, and pottering about on a rather chilly cheerless morning waiting for his number to go up. I think it was Mr Hutchinson who recommended a 'penny dreadful' as the best solace for this bad quarter of an hour of waiting, and certainly the mind should be occupied with something that is not golf.

It is, of course, a stock piece of advice never to give up trying in a medal round. An unexpected three or two towards the end may always transform a bad into a decent score, and apart from that there are days when whole fields are stricken down with absolute impotence, though the weather is fine and there is nothing to account for it but sheer human frailty. It was only last summer that a North Berwick medal was won by a player who, though he had not actually torn up his card, had ceased to take the faintest interest in it some holes before the finish.

The Links of Eiderdown (1934)

Given exactly the right conditions, there are few pleasanter things than a day in bed. We must not be rank imposters; we must be just ill enough to be sure that we shall be nearly well next day or, indeed, quite well so long as we have not to come down to breakfast. We must feel equal not to gross roast beef but to a whiting sympathetically eating its own tail and to a rice pudding, not forgetting the brown sugar. Tobacco, though sparingly indulged in, must not take on the flavour of hay, and though wholly incapable of answering a newly arrived letter, we must be well able to read an old book.

It is best, if possible, to feel some warning symptoms the night before, so that we may be assured that it would be very unwise to get up next morning. Thus we have the joys both of anticipation and of fruition. That such joys are selfish it cannot be denied. The telephone bell rings in the distance and we cannot answer it. The bell rings for luncheon, and there are sounds of scurrying feet as of those late in washing; we are taking a little holiday in that respect and our lunch comes up on a tray. With what heavenly malice do we hear a strange motor-car crunching the gravel under the window. Callers – ha, ha! The new neighbours – ho, ho! We shall be told later that they proved to be very agreeable people and we are perfectly ready to take it on trust. With a last thought of them sitting ranged round the drawing-room, we drift away into a beautiful half-way house between sleep and waking without fearing any of the misery that ensues if we do the same thing in a chair. We shall come to ourselves as bright as a button and ready for another go of *David Copperfield*.

This was my admirable choice last week, and I was so drowsily happy that I found even Agnes 'pointing upward' not unendurable. Only one thing disturbed my serenity. In my warped mind's eye I continually saw golf holes designed on the 'land of counterpane' before me. It is not an uninteresting one, this links of eiderdown, and is laid out on what an ingratiating prospectus would call fine, undulating country. Moreover, by undulating himself in bed the patient can in a moment change the contour of his course. In the ordinary way there is a broad hog's-back ridge extending down the middle of the course. It is doubtless possible to use it in several ways, but I always saw a long plain hole running nearly the whole length of it, slightly downhill with a fall to perdition on either side for the slicer or the hooker. It seemed to me, if I remembered the number aright, rather like the 13th hole at Liphook. There were no bunkers on it of any kind; no 'lighthouses', as the more ferocious of architects scornfully term them, to guide the eye of the tiger and make superfluously wretched the rabbit's life; nothing but a wide expanse on which it would clearly be very difficult to judge distance.

When my eyes dropped to either side of this ridge I felt that I was in another country. Was I at Formby or Birkdale, or perhaps at the 6th hole at Prince's, Sandwich? Here, at any rate, was one of the holes that run along a narrow valley with slopes on either hand – on one side, to be precise, the patient's leg, and on the other the outside edge of the eiderdown. I have always had rather a romantic affection for such holes. I have heard with pain from those same 'highbrow' architects that they are not really good holes, because the mere fact of the banks (which will kick the ball back to the middle) give the player confidence, whereas the architect's duty is to make him hesitating and uncomfortable. I began to think that these irritating views were right; the valley might be narrow, but I felt as if I could drive straight down it, whereas when I looked at the ridge I did not feel nearly so happy.

There were other holes on the course, but they were hardly so satisfactory. There was, to be sure, a big, blind tee shot, to a one-shot hole as I imagined it, over a comparatively noble hill, made by my toes, but somehow it lacked subtlety; and when by a swift piece of engineering I moved the hill to see what the green was like on the far side, it proved flat and featureless. By separating and then adroitly manipulating my two sets of toes it was possible to make a crater green, with visions of the ball running round the side wall and back wall to lie dead at least for an unmerited three. That brought back sentimental memories. I knew a beloved course once that had three such greens running, and many years ago I had three threes running there and won a medal thereby. Still, the sweetness of such threes has a cloying quality. No doubt it is all for the best in the most testing of all possible worlds that there should be no more greens like that nowadays.

To roll over on my side had a disappointing effect on the links. In fact it was obviously not a links any longer, but a mere course: one of those courses on downland which I have the misfortune to dislike, with long, steep slopes, equally tedious to play up or down, and too often adorned with 'gun-platform' greens. When tea came, however, the course took on a new aspect, for the tea-tray was on a bed table and the bed table had four legs. The course was now one cut out of a wood, on which the architect had wisely allowed a solitary sentinel tree or two to remain standing in the middle of the fairway. The valley holes instantly became far more interesting, for each of them had one tree, acting in some sort as a Principal's Nose, for the tee shot, and another, like that capital tree at the first hole at Frilford, bang in front of the green. I spent some time trying to resolve on which side of those trees to go. At one hole it seemed best to try the right-hand line, because if I went to the left I might hook on to the floor, which was clearly out of bounds. At the other hole an exactly converse policy was indicated, but even with the banks to help me the shot was far from easy.

Now I am, as Mr Littimer would say, 'tolerably well' again, and *David Copperfield* is finished. I have no reasonable pretext for not getting up for breakfast, and indeed it is rumoured that there are to be sausages tomorrow morning. The links of eiderdown are fast becoming of the fabric of a dream. I have tried to fix the holes before they elude the frantic clutches of memory and fade away into one another.

A Galley Before the Wind
(1959)

It is a sure sign that summer really is coming in when the members receive the fixture card of their local cricket club. It is never easy to get passionately interested in the beginning of first-class cricket, specially after the squabbling and backbitings of winter and the long, wearisome Test matches have given something of a distaste for the game; but now with this match card and its first date early in May, cricket, and the right sort of cricket, is really coming alive again. On the outside of the card are the stripes of the club colours and its badge; a pleasant little galley sailing before the wind. Look inside and here, as Mr Squeers would say, is indeed richness. First comes the president, who is *de jure* 'Esquire', then the treasurer and secretary who are 'Misters', and then the matches and the four different teams, the Saturday first and second elevens, the Sunday eleven, and the mid-week eleven. For a small town, of ancient lineage to be sure and having very properly a good conceit of itself but no vast number of inhabitants, that is surely a good showing. Cricket cannot be dying in face of those four doughty elevens and their captains and secretaries, and the list is as reviving to the spirits as is the light of the new and engaging pavilion built by the supporters and pools and the really noble ground on which it looks, where once on a chilly day the great F. G. J. Ford made 210 runs batting in a Quidnunc blazer and subsequently insisted on fielding in gloves, contrary to the laws of cricket.

Truly exciting are the names of the opposition. There are first the rival villages against whom a moderate hatred is justifiable. There are the perambulating visitors, wanderers and strollers, and ramblers and nomads. There are two illustrious names known much farther afield, Bluemantles and Martlets. 'Rugby Old Guard' is a title full of thrill and mystery; they must have played for Tom Brown's eleven against old Mr Aislabie and his Marylebone men. Dragons and Gay Cavaliers and Freebooters (who surely used to play polo) are all very 'intriguing'; so are Mediators – do they mediate between the batsman and the bowler? One can 'roam in a crowded mist' of these charming names, until August when six of them come in a row for the cricket week, and on one of those six days an old and faithful friend says he will yet again give a lunch, 'cold but capital – fowls and pies and all that sort of thing', as Mr Jingle remarked.

That Small Colossus:
Hogan at Carnoustie (1953)

As long as golfers talk championship golf, 1953 will be recalled as Hogan's year. Indeed, I think it would have been even if he had not won, so entirely did that small colossus bestride and dominate the tournament.

It was Hogan that sold the tickets in their thousands to the great joy of the authorities and filled the huge park with row upon serried row of shining cars; it was Hogan that produced what was, I think, the greatest crowd of spectators that I ever saw at a championship; and it was Hogan that every single one of them wanted to watch. Hardly anyone there had seen him play before since, when he was here in 1949, he was still too ill to play, and in less than no time anyone with any knowledge of golf came back overawed and abashed by the splendour of his game.

There were to begin with certain local patriots disposed to speak of him as 'Your man Hogan', and to murmur that he might do all manner of things on American inland courses, but let him wait till he comes to play over the great Carnoustie course in a Carnoustie wind. Yet even those parochial critics were soon convinced, for they knew golf and were too honest not to admit that here was such a player as occurs only once in a generation or indeed once in a lifetime. As soon as the one Scottish hope, Eric Brown, had faded away I think the whole of that vast crowd wanted Hogan to win. This is not to say that Dai Rees, the ultimate British hope, who had played most gallantly, would not have been a most popular winner. He certainly would, but the feeling that the best man ought to win – there was no earthly doubt who that was – overrode all other sentiments.

And what a wonderful win it was! He did what Bobby Jones, Hagen and Sarazen had all failed to do at the first attempt. He came here weighed down by his immense reputation, and for the first two rounds his putting was unworthy of him and he seemed to have got the slowness of the greens a little on his nerves so far as he has any nerves. Yet when he once began to take some of the chances which his magnificent iron play gave him, when the putts began to drop so that we said 'Now he's off!', and it was almost a case of in the one class Hogan and in the other class all the other golfers, it was a measure of his quality that having been hard pressed for three rounds, sharing the lead with one very fine player, and having all sorts of others hard on his very heels, he yet managed to win with something like ease.

It is an impossible task to give anything like an impression of the player to those who have not seen him, but one can perhaps pick out one or two points. Hogan stands decidedly upright with his weight rather forward on the left foot and the right foot drawn a little back. He holds his hands decidedly high, the right hand notably far over, and the right wrist almost arched. The swing is rhythmic and easy and not as long as I had expected from the photographs. The club at the top of the swing may in fact go a little past the horizontal, but if so the eye – or my eye – cannot detect it. The impressive part of the swing comes in what the books call the hitting area. Then the clubhead appears to travel with such irresistible speed that it goes right through the ball and far past it before it begins to come up again. He has, incidentally, a good deal of power in reserve, and when he really means to hit out, as he did with his two wooden clubs at the long 6th hole, his length is very great indeed. I suppose, however, it is his iron play – particularly his long-iron play – which is most striking. It is that which gives him so many chances of threes because he hits so appallingly straight. When we were all waiting behind the home green for his iron shot to the 72nd hole and Hogan, no doubt giving the out-of-bounds on the left a wisely wide berth, finished up eight or nine yards to the right of the pin, somebody remarked: 'He's dreadfully crooked, isn't he?' It was a true word spoken in jest. Eight yards to the left or right of the pin was definitely crooked for Hogan.

His putting is, to me at least, the least attractive part of his game, as far as looks are concerned. He has the ball very far forward opposite, or almost in front of, his left foot, with his right foot back, and the whole attitude has something of stiffness. But if ever there was a case of handsome is as handsome does, this is it, for he hits the ball a wonderfully solid blow. The ball does not trickle away at the end of the putt; it goes right in, and when a putt is particularly crucial he seems positively to will it into the hole.

Hogan is a compelling subject, and I have been running on about him like 'a new barrow with the wheel greased'. So I must do scanty justice to others. There is Locke, for instance, who lost the championship but lost it like a champion: his first round of 72 when the north-westerly wind was really blowing hard, was splendid, but he seemed to make just too many inaccurate iron shots. I think I have never seen Rees play better and I think his temperament was in as good order as his golf. His finish of two threes in the second round swept us off our feet with a wave of enthusiasm. I suppose that on the whole he did not play the finishing holes as well as the others. As he came off the green at the end of his last round, having tied with the leaders, but knowing that Hogan would catch them, he exclaimed sadly: 'The 15th and 16th again!'

Eric Brown's two 71s showed his quality. I think he is a little too easily disturbed and not quite philosophical enough to win through at the moment. The one who seems to have the perfect temperament is the young Australian, Peter Thomson. He has now been second twice and he is only twenty-three. As far as anyone can be sure to be a champion he is, and a most worthy and popular one he would be. The South Americans Cerda and de Vicenzo, acquired much merit. Either is just about good enough to win.

Finally, in a quadruple tie for second place was our now old friend Frank Stranahan. He not only played very, very well, but with tremendous courage. He provided one of the most dramatic moments of the tournament in the last round. He seemed out of the hunt so far as winning was concerned, when suddenly it was discovered that he was piling one three upon another and wanted a four at the home hole to be home in 33 and round in 70. The case was altered with a vengeance and when he holed his long putt for a three – he had holed a chip for a three at the very same hole in the morning – and got his 69, it looked as though anything might happen. 'We have seen the putt which won the championship', said one very shrewd friend in an ecstasy of excitement. When we reckoned up what the others had to do it had seemed very possible. 'No, I think Hogan will just do it,' I said, or I think I said, but I didn't think he would do it by four whole strokes. If there was one hole more than another that made that last round of Hogan's it was his three at the 5th, where he holed his chip from a nasty rough place on the back of a bunker. No doubt it was a help, but he was in an unstoppable mood. Carnoustie certainly showed itself a fine, stern examination paper for champions. Only the best could get full marks there.

Afterword
by
Donald Steel

My only meeting with Bernard Darwin came two or three years before he died when arthritis had already become too severe a handicap for him to get out, play, and watch golf as he had enjoyed doing all his life. He had been driven up to the door of the clubhouse at Rye during the annual match between Oxford and Cambridge, given a pink gin, and had found a seat in the corner of a small, crowded bar.

As a former Captain of the club whose links he loved second only to Aberdovey, there was no mistaking who he was. However, on the two days of the University Match, there was always likely to be a slightly strained atmosphere even among his best friends if they happened to have been at Oxford. My light blue Cambridge blazer was therefore welcome evidence that, in me, he had a staunch ally.

If I had been Jack the Ripper, he would still, I believe, have beckoned me over, for on those two days, the Cambridge connection was all that mattered. He was always uninhibitedly partisan although, apart from team events, it was often impossible to detect this fact from his writing. Nevertheless, as his obituary in the Times *of London pointed out, "If Eton or Cambridge were beaten, he never pretended not to regret that the gods of chance had let him down".*

Our meeting only lasted a few minutes, just long enough, in fact, for him to convey the fervent wish that we should win—which happily we did. The following year in an article for Country Life, *which was one of his last, he wrote, "I am, I own, rather frightened of the Oxford tail. I think that Oxford will win, but I hope Cambridge may". A desire to see Oxford's noses rubbed in the dust was uppermost to the last.*

There was never any suggestion then that I should be fortunate enough to join the ranks of writers on golf. My tutor used to delight in telling me that golf isn't so much a game as a disease, but it didn't take long for him to detect that my affection far outstripped any scholastic pretensions. Even after graduating, I had no idea what path to follow. So, in keeping with many who have subsequently found themselves doing what they loved best, my opportunity to follow suit was very much an act of fate.

I didn't go to the lengths of being called to the bar, like Darwin, or of changing professions in midstream as two of the greatest golf-course architects did. Alister MacKenzie, designer of Augusta (with Bob Jones) and Cypress Point, started his working life as a qualified doctor, and Harry Colt, who assisted George Crump in designing Pine Valley, began as an attorney in Hastings.

My great good fortune lay in the establishment of a new London newspaper, the Sunday Telegraph, *and the policy attached to it of recruiting, where possible, a brand new editorial staff—even a complete beginner such as myself. It seems strangely symbolic now that one of my first acts as their golf correspondent was to attend the Memorial Service to Bernard Darwin in the fall of 1961 at St Paul's Church, Covent Garden. St Paul's is known as the actors' church, a block away from the Garrick Club where Darwin was a venerable member and life trustee. The Garrick, whose motto is "All the world's a stage", is a famous meeting place for theatrical and literary figures.*

The vast congregation that included peers, cabinet ministers, judges, generals and golfers from all over Britain knew Darwin far better than I did, but his was a revered name in the world of university golf which I had just left, and his writing had already aroused a deep interest within me. At least, I had identified myself with the great man and, if nothing else, my presence, I felt, was a mark of respect and gratitude.

As someone setting out on a writing career, Darwin was the perfect model, but everyone has to forge his own style, and nobody could emulate him. Sir Walter Simpson and Horace Hutchinson had sown the seeds of golf writing in the last century but it was Darwin who turned it into a respectable and much heralded art. Darwin's writing bore an authority without parallel, based on a profound knowledge and love of the game and an ability to express himself gracefully with an easy turn of phrase even when delivering a stern rebuke.

Leonard Crawley, to whose help and guidance I owe much, as I do to that of Peter Ryde, Herbert Warren Wind, Henry Longhurst, and Pat Ward-Thomas, was most insistent when I joined the Sunday Telegraph *that I add to my library of Darwin's books. As a result, we made regular visits to an old second-hand bookshop in Rye where they could be obtained then for no more than a dollar each.*

What impressed me (and still does) was the freshness of Darwin's writing, his enthusiasm, lack of contrivance and his genuine understanding, developed from his own excellence as a player and his awareness of how golfers feel in various circum-

stances. He never dwelt on failure or was critical when some calamity descended. Of one who missed a tiny putt on an important occasion, he applied the proper perspective. "He may yet be", he said, "a good father and a Christian gentleman".

Nobody could sing the praises better than Darwin but his most priceless gift was in using superlatives only when they were justified. He underwrote rather than overwrote, a lesson to modern newspapermen who feel it necessary to conjure up a crisis or sensation when none exists. In his own words, he always tried "to spread the golfing butter as thinly as possible on the more general bread".

His other enviable ability lay in choosing a subject that would never have occurred to others as meaty enough for expansion into a delightful chapter. That was when the storyteller in him took over. He was a writer of fine English rather more than a purveyor of news. Yet golf was very far from being his only interest. He knew his Dickens backwards. He liked murder cases, Sherlock Holmes, and prizefighting, and was paid the conspicuous compliment of being asked to supply the Introduction to the Oxford Book of Quotations, the first sentence of which reads, "Quotation brings to most people one of the intensest joys of living".

Darwin would have hated writing golf today. He would have despised the interviews and all the commercial razzmatazz. We should be thankful he never had to suffer it. In 1953, when he retired from the Times, *the crystal ball gave little hint of the dramatic developments that lay ahead, but the man on the* Times *responsible for so effectively making the transition that golf's changing world demanded was*

Peter Ryde, whose golfing background was so different from Darwin's.

Whatever tenuous method guided his appointment, or however unpredictable it may have been, it turned out to be inspired. Henry Longhurst was perhaps most people's idea of Darwin's successor, but Sir William Hayley, Editor in Chief of the Times, opted for Ryde on the perfectly logical grounds that, if the paper had relied for years on a supreme figure in the golfing world, why not a complete change?

One sure bet that Hayley backed was the knowledge that Ryde was an excellent writer himself. What Hayley was asking of him was to adapt from his more esoteric duties as Letters Editor and writer of Fourth Leaders and broach horizons where the grass was greener. However, that did not make things any easier for Ryde whose commission could be rated on a theoretical par with taking over from Churchill in 1942 or the actuality of having to succeed Willie Mays as the center fielder for the Giants.

Ryde, who overlapped Longhurst at Charterhouse School before going on to Trinity College, Oxford, joined the Times in 1949 after serving in the war with the Fife and Forfar Yeomanry. He received his journalistic grounding on the Gloucestershire Echo, but his new posting to cover golf was no signal for him to panic. He is blessed with the most equable temperament I have encountered in any man, although it naturally took him a while for him to settle in.

Gerald Micklem recounts that on Ryde's first reporting assignment, the English Amateur championship in which Micklem defeated Ronnie White in the final at Royal Birkdale, Ryde watched the golf *dressed in dark suit, beret, and rolled city umbrella. The beret was later replaced by an assortment of headgear that Ryde had a habit of leaving in equally assorted places. Indeed, when Geoffrey Green, a colleague on the* Times, *reviewed the "World Encyclopedia on Golf" on which Ryde and I collaborated so happily as editors, he described life for Peter as comprising a "continuous game of hunt the thimble." For the benefit of American readers, hunt the thimble is an English party game in which a thimble is hidden and everyone has to look for it.*

Daily golf writing soon introduced a disciplined routine, but one other handicap which Ryde fought for years was, quite literally, anonymity. Until about the mid-1960s, the Times *permitted no writer a by-line—not even Darwin. Articles were headed from Our Golf Correspondent, and, to make matters worse, Ryde inherited the nom de plume for* Country Life *of Water Hazard, a soubriquet that, by printer's error, once became Walter Hazard.*

Not that there is anything anonymous about Ryde when you meet him. Tall enough to have been a Grenadier Guardsman, he became as familiar at the tournaments and championships as the leading players, and the respect and affection for him both as man and writer quickly became genuinely deep-seated and warm. His patience and kindly consideration provided shining contrast to the more ruthless image the world seems to have of journalists. He, too, never missed seeing the funny side of situations which, besides making him such an agreeable and constant companion in all corners of the globe, was a valuable attribute in the madhouse atmosphere under which modern golf writers have to compose and travel.

His desire to help others reflected the gratitude he felt for those who had helped him. Having been born within a couple of miles of Walton Heath and having been a reasonably regular golfer for most of his life, he knew the basics of the game. Indeed, one of the factors which may have clinched his appointment was appearing through the swinging doors of the Times *office in Printing House Square with a bag of clubs over his shoulders. Here, they thought, was a man who at least knew a mashie from a mandolin.*

At the time, Ryde had only once met Darwin and wasn't all that familiar with his writing. His father-in-law, Bill Darlington, the famous drama critic of the Daily Telegraph *for over forty years, rectified the first omission by arranging lunch at the Garrick; and Ryde himself, as he began to get to grips with his new life, soon rectified the second.*

In keeping with all serious golf writers, Ryde found Darwin an invaluable and infallible source of reference, but Ryde's allegiance formed almost Boswellian proportions. If anyone doubts as much, there is lasting proof in the introduction to this very book. It is a quite exceptional analysis, and anyone who has read thus far has almost certainly devoured and digested its delights. Like all good writing, it can be read and re-read.

Weaving together such an accurate and colorful portrayal involved diligent study, but Ryde obviously found Darwin a fascinating subject, although it sadly emphasises the gap that Ryde has left now that he, too, has retired. His insight on Darwin is a notable contribution to the history of the game, and so, like King Henry V, Ryde can claim to have ventured "unto the breach once more", twice emerg-

ing triumphant. Few, if any, could have said the same in similarly searching circumstances.